Crystals — Types, Use and Meaning

Connie Islin

The wonderful world of crystals, the love gifts of Mother Earth, have been revealed to us in this age in which we live, the New Age when we are discovering the hidden knowledge of the Universe.

Almost all of us come into contact with crystals and precious stones in one form or another, as jewelry, or as a tool for healing, fortune telling, or becoming aware of our former reincarnations. These contacts take place both consciously and unconsciously.

This book is a complete guide to the world of crystals; How to use them and learn about associated phenomena such as energy flow, meditation, and healing. 'Crystals' will help you become acquainted with crystals and jewels, learn about the myths associated with them, and find ways to use them for your own practical needs.

Additional chapters address subjects such as crystal balls, pendulums, Chakras, the connection between crystals and colors, and the laying of crystals on the body.

Connie Islin was born in the USA and has written on the subjects of mystics, healing, crystals, and parapsychology. Her books about interpreting dreams and numerology have become bestsellers and have been translated into several languages. She lives in the USA and in Israel, and works as a purchaser of crystals and jewels for the largest chain of mystics shops in Israel. She is also a consultant and lecturer on mystical subjects and alternative medicine.

ASTROLOG COMPLETE GUIDES SERIES

The Complete Guide to Coffee Grounds and Tea Leaf Reading
Sara Zed

The Complete Guide to Palmistry
Batia Shorek

The Complete Guide to Tarot Reading
Hali Morag

Crystals - Types, Use and Meaning
Connie Islin

The Dictionary of Dreams
Eili Goldberg

Meditation: The Journey to Your Inner World
Eidan Or

Playing Cards: Predicting Your Future
Hali Morag

Day-by-Day Numerology
Lia Robin

Using Astrology To Choose Your Partner
Amanda Starr

The I Ching
Nizan Weisman

Crystals

Types, Use and Healing

Connie Islin

Astrolog Publishing House

Astrolog Publishing House

P. O. Box 1123, Hod Hasharon 45111, Israel

Tel: 972-9-7412044

Fax: 972-9-7442714

E-Mail: info@astrolog.co.il

Astrolog Web Site: www.astrolog.co.il

MAY 1 7 2000

© Connie Islin 1998

ISBN 965-494-000-0

Published by Astrolog Publishing House 1999

3 9082 07819 5321

Printed in Israel

10 9 8 7 6 5 4 3

Contents

Crystals and Myths

Stories, legends, and myths relating to crystals and precious stones can be found in the ancient sources of every human culture that has left its mark on history. In the case of Judaism, for example, there are the legends telling of a stone that served as the center for the creation of the entire world. Another legend relates to the "stone of dreams" that Jacob used as a pillow and that enabled him to see the angels. All the apocryphal books include the theme of the connection between God and various precious stones.

Above all, however, myths about crystals relate to the legendary continent of Atlantis. Giant crystals provided the power for Atlantis and were also used to guide people's thoughts. Indeed, it was the abuse of crystals that led to the destruction of Atlantis.

Crystals with special powers are associated with various places around the world, such as Mt. Moriah in Jerusalem, Mt. Sinai (the Tablets of the Covenant), the Bermuda Triangle (where the largest crystal in the world is probably buried under the water), Stonehenge in England, and other similar places. Crystal mines connected to ritual and holy sites are now being discovered all over the world.

In the ancient myths crystals are associated with the

smallest and the greatest of human endeavors. It has been suggested that the pyramids of Egypt, the Temple in Jerusalem, the giant statues on Easter Island, the ziggurats of ancient Babylon, and entire cities in South America may all have been built with the assistance of crystals used to cut and place these giant stones. (The Biblical Shamir for example, has often been associated with diamonds. In South America, pictures have been found of "building supervisors" holding a stick with a large crystal on top emitting a beam. Many other stories of this type can be encountered.)

However, not all the stories relate to building enterprises! Crystals were also used for the most delicate of tasks, including head operations. In archaeological explorations, skulls have been discovered that have undergone complex head operations. Sometimes remnants of crystals have been found in these skulls.

In Atlantis, crystals were used to concentrate energy in a manner similar to present-day lasers. These crystals enabled people to fly, to move from place to place by vaporization, to communicate by means of telepathy, to go on astral journeys, and, in effect, to live for eternity.

Ancient cultures were highly familiar with the structure of crystals, as reflected in their attempts to mimic this structure in their monumental constructions — pyramids, obelisks, ziggurats, and so on. It has been suggested that, with the assistance of giant crystals, these enormous buildings served as a communications system for the entire universe, and as a means of controlling and adjusting climatic conditions.

One well-known myth relates to the capacity of crystals to accumulate almost infinite information and to serve as a ceaseless pool of knowledge. More importantly, crystals enable the central pool of knowledge to be connected directly to human minds, thus fashioning their knowledge, memories, and hopes. Scientists claim that crystal can even store information about molecular structures that are infinite and eternal.

The use of crystals by individuals appears to have developed in Lemuria, the more "human" version of Atlantis. Here crystals were used to meet everyday needs, and to accumulate knowledge, energy, and defensive forces for protection against external threats. Instead of the giant public crystals used in Atlantis, those used in Lemuria were individual, classified according to color and function.

The color properties were used mainly for healing. The properties of the crystal (mainly the number of points or caps) were used for charging or balancing energy. It was here that the map of chakras first appeared and each type of jewel was given its own "region of activity."

In Greece and Rome — to move on to times and places closer to our sphere of understanding — crystals were considered to be the "ice of the gods." Legend has it that crystals arrived in Rome from Olympus, the seat of the gods, and represent the manifestation of the sun — what one might term an "individual sun." Thus personal crystals may be used to intensify or balance the properties of the sun — birth, growth, warmth, cold, vision (including vision of the unknown), and so on.

In Egypt, probably due to the fact that the nation was dependent on the Nile as the source of life, the use of crystals was combined with water. Vessels such as carved crystal goblets and cups were used to transform water into holy or healing water with crystalline properties. In addition, the Egyptians used to grind crystals and mix them with water in order to prepare medicinal potions and other substances.

The shamans — the chosen few of ancient cultures who had the power to consort with the upper beings — used crystals to find and regain harmony between humans and nature. Evidence of this can be found from as far afield as the Far East, Lapland, and among Native Americans. Crystals were used by the shaman as an eye that could see the secrets of nature, connect humans to their Creator, and open the individual's inner eye.

Crystals
in Everyday Use

Crystals have practical, everyday uses, some of which we may know, but many may come as quite a surprise. Many of those involved in the world of precious stones and crystals claim that the difference between those who realize their potential and their capabilities and those who realize only part of their talents and inner and external world lies in an understanding of the use of crystals in everyday life.

Once adapted to your personal energy field and programmed to meet a specific goal, crystals will improve your life beyond all recognition. The use of crystals may be compared to the use of a seeing-eye dog by a blind person. Once the connection is created between the dog and the person, the blind person's life is improved beyond all recognition.

Don't let yourself be blind in the land of the seeing! Use crystals to improve your quality of life! Open your inner eye and see the whole world, layer upon layer, circle within circle.

Crystals are always beautiful precious stones that endure for a long time, do not go to waste, and do not lose their force. All you have to do is look after them and give the stone a chance to open your eyes. We will mention here just a few of the simple and everyday methods whereby you can derive benefit from crystals.

Looking for missing objects

Crystals are extremely useful in trying to find objects you have lost. Hold the crystal in your left hand, and use your imagination to conjure up the image of the object you want to find. After a short while, the crystal will coordinate between your energy frequency and that of the missing object and, without being aware of it, you will go to the place where the object is to be found. [Note that in **personal** use of crystals, there is no need to prepare a crystal pendulum of the type usually employed for these purposes.]

Quitting smoking

Crystal is astonishingly effective for people who want to give up their addiction to cigarettes. All you have to do is to want to quit smoking. Now, every time you feel you want to light a cigarette, take your personal crystal in your left hand and repeat silently to yourself "I want to stop smoking." The crystal will intensify your thought frequency and create a barrier to smoking. Even if you light a cigarette, you will find its taste repulsive.

Dieting to lose or gain weight

When you want to use crystals to improve your control of your eating habits, this can be achieved in two stages:

First, the crystal should be placed in a glass of water two hours before each meal. Before the meal — preferably while you are preparing food for yourself or ordering food — remove the crystal and drink all the water.

When you sit down to eat, hold the crystal in your left hand, or underneath your watch strap or a bracelet on your left wrist. The energy of the crystal will guide you to take the right amount of the right foods to achieve your goal.

This method is mainly effective when the foods being served are in their "natural" state — i.e., not dishes containing complex combinations of cooked foods.

The fresher and simpler the food, the better the crystal will be able to define it for you and guide your sense of hunger.

Addiction of any kind

In order to fight any addiction, from drinking to gambling, from drugs to compulsive sex, the individual should carry his or her own personal crystal around all day, and put it down only on going to sleep.

The personal crystal brings the persons to a higher level of self-awareness. As a result, the individual knows and loves himself or herself more than before. Any form of addiction is based on a negative change in the self. Without crystals, people tend to give up their autonomy in order to secure something else. Crystals help people develop their self-image and be satisfied with themselves as they are, thus enabling them to resist any passion or tendency to addiction of one kind or another.

It is particularly important to note that by balancing the energies they emit, personal crystals prevent people from sinking into deep depression, which is often the cause of addiction.

The search for material success

Crystals promote sober consideration of all aspects of life and add a touch of intuition, the main characteristic we need when making business decisions. If you have ever wondered why every luxury stationery shop has a section selling "executive toys" such as crystal paper-weights, statuettes, or stamps, this is why.

Taking a crystal in the left hand when you need to make a decision helps "sharpen" the individual's senses. Taking a few seconds or minutes to reflect before making a decision, while maintaining contact between the crystal and the individual, greatly improves the quality and accuracy of the decision.

You can't argue with success!

Enhancing your sexuality

Crystals can be used to enhance any individual's sexuality, and to improve the sexual relationship between partners using personal crystals (each of the partners must have their own crystal for this to work!).

In this case, the personal crystal should be worn on a strap attached to the wrists or ankles (polarically placed for men or women). The crystal is used to restore virility for men, and to enable women to recognize their own sexuality and their ability to reach orgasm, to overcome sexual inhibitions, to cope with crises, and even to improve their fertility.

If both partners use crystals, they must coordinate the type and strength of the crystals used, and they must wear them in complementary positions on the body.

Use in ceremonies, mass meditation, conventions, or awareness gatherings

Routine and extraordinarily effective use has been made of crystals since ancient times in holding ceremonies or gatherings based on spirituality or mental awareness. By their very definition, such events bring together people with considerable and diverse energies.

When the participants wear crystals, or when crystals are present at the meeting place (for example as part of sacred or ritual objects), a balance is created between these different energies, without any of the participants being harmed by the effort involved.

By way of example, if everyone who came to a court building were required to carry a crystal, I am sure that the atmosphere in these institutions would be improved greatly.

It might also be worth sending each of our legislators a personal crystal; this would surely create a new atmosphere of peace and tranquility in our government institutions!

Connections between people and pets

Crystals have been and still are used to open channels of energy communication between humans and pets. This explains why knights used to place crystals in their horses' saddles, or why hunting dogs carry crystals in their collars. When a pet carries a crystal, its adaptation or properties are those of the human, and it connects the person to his or her pet.

When a horse or dog dies, the stone may be purified and used to create a connection with another pet. Most people, however, prefer to bury the stone with the pet with whom it created a connection.

Healing through sound

Any type of healing that uses sound, such as moaning to release feelings of mourning, noises designed to develop and treat the fetus, etc., must take place in the presence of a personal crystal that transmits and balances the sounds according to the patient's energies. Trying to use sound as a tool for healing without crystals is almost completely ineffective.

Protection from radiation, electric current, or various energy frequencies

Humans live in environments in which energy waves control various forms of radiation. At any moment, humans both emit and absorb hundreds, or possibly even thousands, of different types of radiation, some of which are harmful.

Since the human body is composed mainly of water, which easily absorbs and is influenced by radiation, we must protect ourselves as much as we can from radiation — known and conscious or unknown.

Crystals are the simplest and most effective way to repel negative radiation and seal the body, spirit, and soul to them. Just try it! It can't do any harm, and the benefit could considerable in terms of your quality of life and life expectancy.

We have suggested here some ways that crystals may be used for everyday purposes, even by people who are not devoted advocates of the properties of crystals. Good luck!

Selecting Your Personal Crystal

Selecting the right crystal for the right moment is an extremely important point. How do we know what type of crystal we should choose, and which stone of this type is the right one for us?

We can ask an expert or consult with people who understand this field. Another way is to read books and study the subject of personal precious stones and personal crystals. These are both possibilities, but we have a much easier and more convenient proposal:

Just listen to your inner voice — the sense of intuition or "gut feeling" that each person has inside them. This inner voice or inner eye will lead you to choose the right stone for you.

What this means in practical terms is that you should stand opposite the selection of stones and crystals. Reach out your hand and take the first stone to which it is drawn. Lift up the stone; hold it and feel it. If a connection is made between the person and the stone, it will feel as if the stone was born in your palm!

Another possibility is to use sparks of light. Place the different types of stones, or different stones of a single type, on a table and cast light on them (candle-light is best, but not essential). One of the stones will reflect a spark back to you. That's your stone!

When you pick up the stone, make sure you use your left hand, even if you are left-handed. If the stone feels comfortable in your hand, look at it. Try to see its color — not only with your regular eye, but also with your inner eye. Try to connect the stone with some sound that it reminds you of. Try to use the skin of your hand to feel the stone. Remember that your palm is controlled by the chakra of fine and sensitive sensations.

Crystals can be thought of as snowflakes. The potential variety of samples is infinite. Just as no two snowflakes are identical, neither are any two crystals. Each stone has its own texture, shine, radiation range, and "personality." People classify stones according to type, size, color, shape, lucidity, and so on. This is the easy way out, and actually the only way. We can't classify stones according to "personality," because each stone has its own personality. Each individual must try to find the stone whose personality or radiation range matches their own personality. The only person who can do this is the individual themself — the one who uses the stone according to his intuitive sense.

It is important to recall that someone who is sensitive to crystals will always react to some extent to the range of a particular stone. Think about relations between humans: there are many people for whom we feel something, but then there is that someone for whom we feel something special! What we are looking for is each person's "special" stone.

The stone you hold in your hand must meet two main requirements. First, it must feel "good," without any reservations. If you feel even the slightest unpleasant sensation — a prickling, burning, or heavy feeling — find another stone! The second requirement will be obvious to anyone who has already been lucky enough to find his own personal stone. The stone must "live" in your hand. In other words, you should feel as though there were a tiny living creature, a puppy perhaps, in your palm, not an inanimate stone. The stone "comes alive" in your hand — that's what you must feel.

In order to achieve the best contact you can with the stone, there must be complete harmony. It is true that you may be able to get along with a stone even if there is not complete harmony (just as we can get along with people in the absence of complete harmony). But complete harmony will achieve the best results. This is why it is important to try to find the most suitable stone for you personally — **the one using the stone!**

Bear in mind that every stone has its own pace of adaptation. With some stones, you will be able to feel the harmony (or the lack of it) from the first moment. In other cases, it may even take weeks to be sure whether or not there is harmony between the stone and yourself.

With some crystals, the size or cut of the stone is of

importance, while in other cases this is unimportant.

A good way to decide about a particular stone is to think about an animal you are particularly fond of. If you have a cat you are very attached to, imagine the stone as a little kitten. If the imagery "works," that means you have made a good choice.

Another more complex method is suitable for people who have studied about the use of stones and are aware of their body, soul, and spirit. Hold the stone that you feel may be "your" stone in your left hand. Now hold your right hand in a fist, with the thumb sticking up. With the pad of your thumb, press one of the points along the main axis of the chakras — the axis passing from the bridge of your nose to the pubic bone. There are 16 appropriate pressing points; everyone knows one or more of these points, since they are sensitive to the touch. If you do not know the points, use your right thumb to press the following points, in this order: the bridge of your nose, upper lip, lower lip, the small triangle at the base of your neck, and so on down to the pubic bone. This will help you find your "open" points. At one or more points you will feel a "current" pass through your body (sometimes accompanied by a painful sensation). Press this point for some time with your right thumb while holding the stone in your left hand. If the stone is suitable, you will feel that the radiation or fluctuation of the stone reaches your right thumb — the fluctuation of the stone blends with the fluctuation of your body. If you feel this kind of current, the stone is the right one for you!

Placing Crystals On Your Hand and Body

Even today, when the use of crystals is widespread and is becoming part of everyday life, most crystals are used as jewelry, particularly rings. It has been estimated that 90% of all crystals and precious stones are used in the form of jewelry of one kind or another.

Crystal jewelry is extremely powerful. The field of radiation of the crystal ranges from ten centimeters to 1.5 meters, depending on the type of crystal, its size, and the surrounding environment. It goes without saying, then, that a crystal worn on the body has a strong influence on the person wearing it.

We are not always aware of the influence exerted by the crystals we wear. Sometimes we wear crystals just for their beauty, and not because of their special properties.

However, as soon as we open our consciousness to crystals, we must learn the right way to wear jewelry — on our fingers, hands, or other parts of our body — in order to direct the energy flow between the crystal and the human in the best possible manner.

First, we must realize that our bodies have a receiver side and a transmitter side. To compare our bodies to a telephone, the left side, and **the hand** in particular, is the receiving side. **The left side is the best receiver of influences from the environment, including radiation from crystals.** In other words, the left side is the side that is sensitive to the environment. When we want to bring something into our bodies — not by means of therapy, healing, or the use of crystals, but by semi-conscious uses, such as wearing jewelry— then the left side is the side that best receives things from the environment into our bodies.

The right side is the transmitter side: the side that emits radiation. This is the side that is active and influences the environment (by contrast with the passive, receiving left side). **If someone wants to radiate particular properties more strongly, the right side is the one that transmits to the environment.**

As we all know, the hand plays an extremely important part in human life, since the hand is the basic organ people use in their physical contact with the environment. According to this approach, the fingers are channels. Each channel receives and transmits mainly a specific property (which is enhanced and intensified by certain crystals).

If you compare the names of the fingers and knuckles in palmistry (Jupiter, Saturn, the Sun Finger, Mercury, etc.), and the properties attributed to the various fingers in astrology, with the properties attributed to each finger in the use of crystals, **you will find a striking but totally unsurprising similarity**.

It is important to understand that wearing crystals on the fingers in the form of a ring is the most widespread, convenient, and persistent way to use crystals. Many rings stay on the finger throughout the day. It is not difficult to appreciate, then, that rings are of cardinal importance in the correct use of crystals. Everyone is familiar with special rings made from crystal which can be worn in order to enhance a particular characteristic in the individual.

Our subject here is confined to the way to make sure that the relevant quality, the finger or body part, and the crystal will be coordinated in order to maximize the benefit to the individual. Bear in mind, though, that the type of metal in which the crystal is embedded and the combination of several crystals in a single piece are also significant factors.

To sum up:

Remember that the left side receives the radiation of a particular property, while the right side transmits that property (or activates it). However, the different functions of both sides of the body or both hands are completely symmetric.

The thumb is the one finger on which we should not wear jewelry or rings. The reason is that the thumb symbolizes willpower or desire (just as in palmistry). The thumb is considered a special finger due to its ability to change its direction relative to the body.

The thumb, as the symbol of willpower, could be seen as something belonging to the innermost parts of the human, both in receiving and in transmiting this quality. Since this is an inner property that essentially reflects or realizes other properties, it is not customary to charge this property through the use of crystal jewelry.

The index finger (next to the thumb) receives messages from the environment and influences the individual's charisma, goals, aspirations, and desires. It is important to appreciate that the energy of the crystal worn on the index finger leads to the reception of inner messages from the conscious and subconscious ego, and, at the same time, leads to the transmission of these messages from the right side into the inner conscious self or out to the environment.

The middle finger receives and transmits in the field of intuition or, more broadly, enlightenment and training. This finger has considerable ability to receive and transmit feelings.

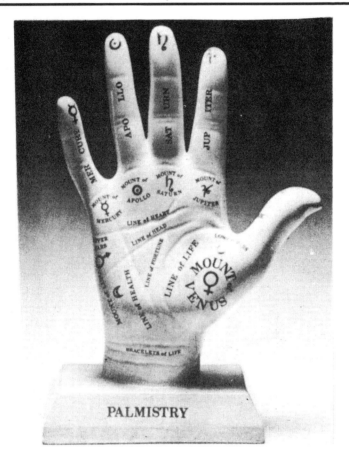

PALMISTRY

The ring or fourth finger (next to the small finger) relates to the sphere of creativity. It receives creative impulses and properties and transmits them outward. Note that the entire field of **love** and romance is included in this finger (and note where you wear your engagement or wedding ring!)

The small finger is the finger of change and new paths. On the left hand, radiation will enhance the individual's ability to cope with new challenges. On the right hand, it will help the wearer to motivate other people and energies in order to achieve the desired change.

A ring worn on the appropriate finger effectively functions as a highly powerful energy source, receiving or transmiting as the individual chooses, and targeted on a specific property. **Remember that the difference between inward or outward movement depends on the hand — left or right.**

The following list details the crystals and precious stones most commonly used as insets in rings, according to the finger:

Index finger — messages
Lapis lazuli: to enhance knowledge, intellect, logic, and memory.
Garnet: to enhance self-confidence and humanity.
Moonstone: to enhance self-love.
Mother-of-pearl: to enhance love of others.
Carnelian: to enhance the impulse to achieve goals and self-realization.
Turquoise: for relaxation and calming.
Sodalite: for mental tranquility.
Chrysolite: to blend in consciousness with the environment.

Middle finger — intuition

Amethyst: to enhance creativity or inspirational capacity.

Sapphire: to focus on noble goals.

Ruby: to radiate "inner beauty"; to expose the pure and conscious soul.

Ring finger — creativity

Ruby: to enhance the ability to recognize beauty.

Diamond: to strengthen ties of love.

Emerald: to promote innovations and new ideas.

Tiger eye: to direct creativity to realization.

Cat's eye: to complement creativity with actual creation.

Moonstone: to share love.

Turquoise: to blend intuition and practicality.

Opal: to engender humane action.

Small finger — change

Pearl: to enhance organizational and orderly capacities.

Turquoise: to calm tension and nerves.

Aventurine: new opportunities.

If you define the goals and impulses that shape your behavior and select the appropriate stone, ring, and finger, on the right or left hand (and sometimes simultaneously on both hands, for example when we are looking for love and for a connection of love, and need both reception and transmission) — you will have made a huge step in the conscious use of crystals.

The fingers are sensitive channels, and the energies that flow through them can exert powerful influences. The simple rules outlined above should prevent mishaps and improve your everyday use of crystals.

We have seen that careful attention must be paid to the correct side of the body, in terms of reception or transmission, and to the correct finger on each hand in order to direct the power of the stone to the most appropriate channel.

Most precious stones are worn in the form of jewelry, and in this sphere rings offer a clear advantage. However, many items of jewelry need not be worn only on the fingers. It is important to choose the right stone for the right part of the body in order to exploit its positive value to the maximum.

The body is divided into a number of regions which should be recognized in order to choose the right stone for your purpose.

First, there are two other areas, apart from the hands, where the rule **left = receive, right = transmit** also applies. These are the arms and the feet (from approximately three centimeters above the ankle right down to the toes). These areas obey the law of energy reception from stones: extreme sensitivity on the left side, and the emission of energy and initiation of activity on the right side.

The toes also carry parallel characteristics to the fingers. The big toe should not carry stones, while the other toes have the same properties as the comparable fingers. This method requires a considerable level of spirituality, since the energy channel to the center of the body is long and convoluted. This method is not widely used and beginner users need not relate to these distinctions.

In addition to these two areas, the central part of the human body is divided into the following regions, from the top down:

The head includes two centers which are in some ways analogous to chakras. On the forehead, there is a spot which stimulates cognitive creativity, accelerates the activities of the brain, and directs the individual to correct thought.

Parallel to this point, and at the back of the head, in the sunken area that anyone can feel above their neck, there is a point that charges people with active energy, contributing to their resilience and perseverance. (Incorrect charging of this area leads to a stiff neck in both physical and mental terms.)

The large triangle or upper triangle is a region extending from the lower part of the neck through to the middle of the chest, as defined by the chest bones. This region influences love, desire, impulses, and wishes. This is an important region which may be influenced by combining a number of stones. It is important to allow the stone free movement in this region (e.g., by means of a chain), since the influence is not pinpointed, but extends across a wide area.

The waist or belt line is a region that influences activity and ambition. This region divides the upper and lower parts of the body and extends right around the body, like a belt. This belt is sometimes compared to the zodiac, and the individual's star sign may be positioned relative to the belly button. In such cases, a precious stone may be placed in the sphere of a particular star sign around the belt, thus providing the stone with a convenient opening for transferring energy. In this case, of course, the individual must know what property they wish to improve and what the appropriate stone and star sign are.

The lower or pubic triangle lies opposite the triangle under the neck. Note that unlike the usual Star of David, these two triangles both point in the same direction — down. This region influences the individual's vitality and sexuality.

The arms are used mainly for the realization or implementation of other properties. When we want to receive energy in order to act — the left side is appropriate. When we wish to help someone else to act or make them act — the right side should be used. The best part of the arm is the wrist.

The legs, particularly the feet and ankles, provide a foundation and support. Here, too, the left/right principle should be recalled.

We will now be able to understand the way different people from different cultures use jewelry. Stones are used not only for decoration or for the accumulation of wealth, but more importantly as an energy store directed to a particular goal and a specific part of the body.

Almost everyone wears a watch, but some people may feel uncomfortable with a particular watch. Why is this so? The answer is that some watches include quartz "stones," and for some people quartz on the left hand creates discomfort and unnecessary tension.

A bracelet serves as an effective and useful way of dissipating tension, balancing energies and even healing certain illnesses. Naturally, the type of metal or other material from which the bracelet is made, and the stone or stones it bears, must be appropriate to the person and the illness. Turquoise, coral, or ivory bracelets on the left wrist, for example, calm high levels of tension.

It goes without saying that bracelets are effective mainly because they are positioned on a natural energy channel — the pulse, symbolizing the blood system.

In ancient times, warriors in Egypt and Babylon used to wear bracelets bearing personal stones before going to war. These stones protected the warriors' lives. When they captured an enemy, the first thing they would do was to take their protective bracelet.

In general, we can state that the right bracelet with the right stone will always protect the physical body and strengthen the energy it contains.

A chain or necklace worn around the neck may be used for a wide range of purposes. It is also possible to place a number of coordinated stones on the chain. A chain of pearls, for example, including a little red coral, enhances self-confidence. The location of the stones may be controlled by shortening or lengthening the chain or by combining a number of chains.

For the head, **earrings** studded with precious stones may be used, since the ears are a highly-sensitive part of the body. (In fact, the ear is a "map" of the individual's body and soul, or a miniature map of the whole body). Care should be taken not to charge the ear with energy from excessively strong stones such as opal or lapis lazuli, since the high receptive capacity of the ear and the proximity of the two regions in the head leads to an accumulation of energy that may "drug" body and soul. Earrings made from quartz, sapphire, jade, tiger eye, sapphire, garnet, or diamond are the most appropriate.

Stones may also be used through the eye or nose. In ancient Egypt, Babylon and Israel, powder made from precious stones (kohl, for example) was used to color the eyes or nostrils. This is the best way to help energy penetrate the "third eye" in the center of the forehead.

A chain may be used to position various stones in the center of the forehead, particularly when the individual wishes to enhance his or her personality and consciousness. The center of the forehead is an important part of the body. In India, this place was chosen for the largest and most expensive stone — diamond, sapphire, or ruby. Bear in mind that this is a powerful point; incorrect use may distort the individual's inner balance of energy.

Jewels and precious stones placed on the head by means of a **crown**, diadem, or other means of attachment to the hair require a profound understanding of the powers of crystals and precious stones. It is important to learn about the balance between different stones. This is a sensitive region, particularly in terms of inner consciousness. When we bear in mind that some crowns may contain 300 stones or more, it is easy to appreciate the tremendous radiation absorbed by a person who uses a crown.

Belts studded with precious stones, particularly ones chosen to match the individual's star sign, exert a strong influence. Belts are particularly effective for charging the wearer with energy, vitality, and self-confidence. Stones such as turquoise or various types of agate may be used, as may shell or red stones (red stones used in this manner improve the blood circulation).

In many cultures we find a tradition of jewelry worn on the **ankle**. Often a man and a woman will wear identical jewels with identical stones if they wish to strengthen the relationship between them. Quartz, jasper, or agate may be used for this purpose. This part of the body also protects the wearer from physical or emotional addiction and enhances stability in all areas of life.

Precious stones carried **in the pocket** mainly effect the lower triangle region, but may have other effects since people tend to touch with their hands whatever they have in their pockets. When using a special stone for a particular purpose, the preferred method is usually to carry it in the pocket.

Precious stones may be used in many and varied ways. For example, some people recommend that powder made from a precious stone, or small stones, be placed in the shoe.

As is well known, the foot is a strong receiver of influences from the environment. A stone in this part of the body serves both to isolate the foot from evil influences and to filter beneficial properties.

Becoming acquainted with the different parts of the body and the effect each stone has on each part and side of the body is the first step toward correct and effective use of the power of crystals and precious stones.

Pure Quartz:
The Father of Crystals

When we think of crystals, the first picture that comes to mind is pure, transparent quartz. Indeed, if we walk into the right store and ask for a "crystal" we will invariably be offered some type of pure quartz.

Quartz is a crystal composed of silicon dioxide found throughout the world and well-known for its ability to transmit waves with precision, as well as for its healing and meditation properties. Even people who do not believe in crystals are attracted to the appearance of pure quartz, a combination of natural glass and the shine of diamonds.

Not for nothing has quartz been referred to as the "father" of crystals. **Indeed, quartz and crystals are synonymous!**

What is special about pure quartz is the large number of forms it may take. **Yet all these forms obey one common principle**: a crystal always has a six sides prism with pyramidal terminations.

Basic quartz always includes six facets which are always completely equilateral and concentric relative to the center of the crystal. A perfect quartz has six sides or facets and creates a perfect prism.

In addition to the six facets, a quartz includes two other parts: the top surface and the bottom surface. When a quartz is found in "Mother Earth," either or both of these surfaces is usually attached to the rook. Toward the connection point, the six sides unite in a point like the point of a pencil. Such points may sometimes be found on both sides of the crystal.

The quartz is the perfect manifestation of a crystal. The six points are analogous to the six chakras in the human body. The point or tip is the seventh chakra, which connects us to Mother Nature.

Pure quartz appears in a variety of forms, each of which has its own name and properties. The different forms of quartz usually derive from each other: a single-pointed quartz may become a double-pointed quartz, and so on.

The following list details various types of pure quartz **according to the shape of the points and the cut of the crystal**.

Single-pointed quartz (Single Terminated)

Six sides converging in a single point like the tip of a sharpened pencil. This is an extremely common type of quartz, and everyone who is involved in crystals has at least one such stone. Some people call this crystal a Generator, since it is used to charge positive energy and remove negative energy. Used in healing. Care should be taken during use not to draw too much negative energy toward the crystal, since this may affect the user.

Double-pointed quartz (Double Terminated)

Six sides creating two points on either side of the quartz, like a pencil sharpened at both ends. Very common, and used mainly to balance and connect different energies.

The two points of these crystals need not be of identical size (sometimes one side has a clear point, while the other has a number of points). A crystal with two identical points is ideal for balancing the energies of both members of a couple.

Right-handed or left-handed quartz

A single-pointed quartz in which the "point" is not small, but leaves a wider face. When the wider face veers to the right, the quartz is said to be right-handed, and vice-versa. Quartz of this type is useful when addressing problems that require healing or energy charging (remember that in healing the hand used by the healer is of importance). These crystals are intended for use by professional healers or people with extensive experience in using crystals.

Quartz cluster

A surface from which a large number of quartzes emerge, usually single-pointed. This surface is extremely powerful, since the crystals charge and strengthen each other. When placed in the center of a room, they influence the entire room and all those who enter it. Ideal for group meditation. Also used to purify other stones.

Tabular quartz

This is a form of single-pointed, double-pointed, or cluster quartz which gives the appearance of having been "squashed" forcefully. It looks like a plate, with just a few quartzes protruding.

Tabular quartz is extremely powerful, as if the force had been compacted during the squashing process. Although tabular quartz is not as attractive as other types of quartz, it is powerful and useful particularly for achieving balance between different people.

Herkimer quartz
(Herkimer diamond)

A very short double-pointed quartz with points resembling those of a diamond. Used as a personal stone. Very effective in enabling the user to penetrate his or her subconscious, particularly through dreams. Not recommended for men who suffer from depression or sexual problems. Although personal and loving, this stone may, if inappropriate for a particular person, cause aggravation and disrupt inner balance.

Crater quartz

A quartz of any type in which we can see a small hole, usually parallel to the center. Sometimes the sides of the hole may also show the six-sides structure of the quartz. These are quartzes in which a second quartz was once embedded but came loose, leaving behind an empty space. This space invites users to "penetrate" the crystal, and is therefore only appropriate for those who are experienced and well-versed in the use of crystals. An excellent stone for enlightenment, meditation, or for healing people suffering from severe crises.

Pregnant quartz (baby quartz)

We often find a quartz inside which, or close to which, another smaller quartz can be seen. These smaller quartzes are in a stage of development. They begin when an ordinary quartz contains a "baby" quartz (or a number of babies). Over the course of time, the baby quartz breaks out, continues to develop itself, and eventually separates from the mother quartz (which then remains, at least temporarily, in the form of a crater quartz).

These quartzes are appropriate for use by people who are familiar with the nature and uses of crystals, and are mainly employed when they wish to deal with a specific problem or field.

Quartz pencil

A single- or double-pointed quartz pencil is a very

long, thin quartz. Due to its structure, the quartz focuses its energy, and is therefore also called a Laser quartz. The main property of this quartz is to focus energy on a small area. It is therefore used in healing to mend defects and holes in the aura. Some people also call these quartzes "quartz scalpel," analogous to a scalpel in conventional medicine. Such quartzes must be used with extreme caution.

Chakri quartz

A quartz with an extra, seventh face. The property of this quartz is that the faces are not of identical size. This type of crystal is excellent for use in communication and in contacts with other worlds. The chakri quartz (named after the seven chakras in the human body) may appear in various forms according to the energy flow within the crystal. The main forms are those which transmit energy inward and outward.

Phantom quartz

A quartz inside which mysterious shapes (such as pyramids or Stars of David) or figures may be seen. Relatively expensive. These quartzes are used according to the figure inside and the needs of the user. These are important stones in reincarnation or out-of-body experiences. A very personal stone. Sometimes the shape inside the quartz may develop and change over its own lifetime (and that of its owner).

Round quartz

This is a circular quartz constituting a natural version of the "crystal ball." Due to its spherical and cyclical shape, this quartz is used for prophesying, group communication, problems of pregnancy and fertility, and so on. As a natural crystal ball, this type of quartz is more powerful than the usual manufactured crystal ball. The round quartz may, of course, be shaped and designed.

This ball often takes the appearance of a **quartz egg**, which is used similarly to a round quartz or quartz ball. A crystal egg is used for individual rather than group purposes.

Staircase quartz

This type of structure is composed of a quartz including a large number of crystals, with a cell-like structure. This quartz is difficult to use, and stores cosmic and human knowledge. Some people break this quartz up and use the separate pieces. This quartz sometimes appears in a bush-like form — the **branched quartz**.

Colored quartz

Quartz often includes various colors; the best known is the wonderfully beautiful **rainbow quartz**.

Bear in mind that there are actually dozens of stones from the quartz family that are colorful and attractive. This section is confined to pure, clear quartz. Stones such as smokey quartz, blue quartz, red phantom quartz, tourmaline quartz, and so on, are to be treated as separate stones, not as part of the category of clear quartz.

Pure, clear quartz is the main crystal found in the kits of healers or crystal enthusiasts. Some quartz crystals are used in their own right, while others serve to charge, purify, strengthen, or balance other stones.

If you are just beginning to use crystals, pure, clear quartz, in one form or another, is the first stone you should study and — above all — feel. "Father quartz" is the first step in the wonderful world of crystals.

When you enter a shop where crystals are sold, you will often find other types of quartz with local names given by a salesperson or healer. This is of no particular importance — all the various kinds of quartz are related in one way or another to the basic forms. The most important thing is **the connection created between yourself and the crystal**, not its name or classification.

When you purchase a quartz and want to use a training book to guide you in its use, try to define the quartz according to the list in this chapter, since these definitions are the ones most commonly encountered in such books. Note that a particular quartz may be included in two categories (for example, a double-pointed quartz and a colored quartz; or a laser quartz with an embedded baby).

Crysal Balls

No discussion of crystals can fail to mention the world of crystal balls, which we know mainly as instruments for clairvoyance, spells, and magic. The crystal ball is the oldest and most widespread example of the use of crystals' special properties.

It is a fact that crystal balls, made from different stones and in varying sizes, have been found in every human culture that has ever been studied: Ancient Egypt, Israel, Greece, Rome, Crete, Syria, the British Isles, France, Germany, Peru, Easter Island, Japan, Australia, Siberia, Turkey, North America, South America and Latino America. Hardly a place can be found where archaeological excavations have been held without uncovering crystal balls preserved in their entirety through hundreds of generations, or fragments of crystal balls.

In South America, the cultures that follow the ancient Inca and Maya ways use rounded glass-like stone for fortune-telling. In the East, crystal balls were known as "the windows of the gods." The Dalai Lama has different crystal balls for a wide range of religious purposes. In India, people believe that a person who looks into crystal ball develops his or her inner being; here, crystal ball is known as "the stone of enlightenment."

At various altars found in South America and the Far East, crystal balls serve as a corridor into the "final eternal void."

We know that soothsaying using crystal balls was already commonplace twenty thousand years ago. The main use of crystal is as a window between the world we live in and the world of eternity, past and future, and on to higher worlds than our own.

Crystal balls (the generic term for the balls people use for fortune-telling) are now made mainly from pure quartz, so that crystal and quartz have become synonymous. In the past, however, balls were also made from other stones, such as beryl, aquamarine, emerald, and other members of the quartz family. These balls are sometimes made from crystal balls (mainly quartz) which have a naturally spherical shape, though in most cases the crystal is processed into a ball-like shape.

Evidence has been found proving that crystal balls were used in Biblical times, in the Greek, Roman, and Persian empires, and in medieval Europe. However, the greatest single inspiration to use crystal balls in the world familiar to us came from John Dee, an astrologer and magician in the court of Queen Elizabeth. Using his famous crystal ball, he managed to contact an Upper Being that granted him a rare ability to predict the future, including a knowledge of a unique language taught to him by one of the angels, which he used to write down all his prophecies. John Dee's crystal ball was made of quartz (which has been identified as smokey quartz) and had a slightly misshapen egg-like form. A crystal ball supposed to be that of John Dee is on display in the British Museum, but no one is permitted to use it.

In the footsteps of John Dee, crystal balls became commonplace in England, France, and Germany, and were credited with properties of fortune-telling, good luck, and healing. These balls were very expensive and were carefully passed down from generation to generation within the family (to the oldest son, or to a daughter who possessed "magical" powers). In size, these crystal balls ranged from olive size to enormous balls weighing hundreds of pounds.

It is also important to recall that despite the term "crystal ball," most of these objects are not actually spherical balls. They may appear in the form of eggs, plates, mirrors, or statues, with the form of skulls (mainly for the purpose of mental awareness), fists (to secure power and might), hearts (for love), and so on. In many other cases, crystals ball are fashioned in the shape of gods, people, or animals.

For sexual purposes, crystal balls in the shape of the male or female sexual organs are used. In the Canaanite temples, for example, there were ritual prostitutes who granted the pleasures of their body to those who came to the temple. These women had phallic-shaped crystals through which they would receive the gods' acceptance of the sacrifice. They also used these crystals to purify their body.

The fashioning of crystal balls into figures became a

highly sophisticated craft, and some of the creations are considered to be real works of art. (We must also not forget the natural statues, which will be discussed below. These are figures or forms that show no signs of carving or sculpting. Such crystals are found in the form of eggs, fists, skulls, etc.)

The following are some examples of the use of crystal balls in cultures that are familiar to us:

* King Saul went to visit the soothsayer in Ein Dor, as we know from the Bible. The Hebrew name Ein Dor means "the eye of the ball" — i.e. the eye that sees through a ball. Thus the Bible gives us an explicit example of predicting the future through the use of a crystal ball.

* The noble women of ancient Rome carried a crystal ball due to the belief that crystal was an eternal form of ice that would cool their body during the summer. They believed that crystal originated from the ice on the peak of Mt. Olympus, the seat of the gods.

* Buddhist monks wear a crystal ball around their necks to enable them to communicate with various beings from the world of the dead.

* In various cultures, young men and women with prophetic skills would receive clients in the temples, using

crystal balls to establish communication. The person asking the question would gaze into the ball and think the question silently; then the young man would take the ball and see the answer in it.

* At various magic ceremonies, crystal balls are used by the magician like a candle, sword, or cross in his work.

* In order to achieve complete physical and mental cleanliness, a crystal ball is used for a "test." After a ceremony of purification and cleansing, a crystal ball is taken in the hand. If the ball clouds over, the process must be repeated.

* The combination of a crystal ball and the sun or moon is extremely powerful. In the case of the sun, the person places themself between the sun and the ball. In the case of the moon, the ball is raised up toward the moon (preferably during a full moon).

* According to astrologers, crystals and crystal balls are used for communication with the moon.

* In ancient Egypt, people used to put fragments of crystals or crystal balls on the forehead of the dead, at a point equivalent to the third eye, in order to open a channel of communication between the living and the dead.

* In the East, small crystal balls were used to enhance sexual desire and fertility in women (this is the origin of the Chinese "love eggs"). In other places, crystal balls were used to induce abortion.

* Archaeological excavations in the Maya civilization have discovered human sacrifices whose hearts have been removed and replaced with crystal balls. Even the robbers who have plundered the tombs dared not remove the balls!

A fascinating aspect seen in different myths relates to the connection between mythical dragons or snakes and crystal balls (and precious stones). Many statues and pictures show crystal balls held in the mouths of dragons or snakes or carried on their bodies. The choice of these powerful mythical beasts as the guardians of the crystal balls reflects their importance.

Many works of art are comprised partly of crystal balls and partly of a base, a decoration of an animal, carved and sculpted in crystal. Most of these objects come from the Far East. This is an art form requiring the utmost precision, and reflecting a combination of all the different beliefs relating to crystals.

The working instructions for the artist are detailed in the extreme: He must purify his body and soul before beginning work. He is always to ensure that the ball is located in the center of the work; some refer to the crystal ball in such works as "the heart of the dragon" — i.e. the essence of the work. We should recall that in the Oriental languages, crystal is referred to as "dragon's blood," "dragon's heart," or "dragon's tears." In fact, the legends claim that crystals were created from the saliva of dragons. (We should mention that similar legends can be found relating to precious stones, particularly diamonds and sapphire, which were guarded by dragons and poisonous snakes. These, too, were kept in the creatures' mouths and protected by poisonous saliva. Such legends are found, for example, in the Jewish and Islamic traditions.)

Humans discovered crystals some twenty thousand years ago. It is reasonable to assume that the first crystals were found in stones washed down by water, which stood out because of their special shine and complex shape against the background of simple river pebbles.

Over hundreds or thousands of years, the flow of water polished the crystals, which probably had the form of polished eggs (such crystals can still be found in the debris of rivers). Sometimes crystals were found which had only recently reached the river — these would have sharp protrusions that reflected light in strange ways.

When people began to collect crystal eggs or balls, they felt from the outset that something was going on within them. Suddenly a connection was forged between themselves and the stone, or between themselves and other beings. Unlike other stones, such as flint, which was used in manual labor, crystal was used for the labor of the soul. People suddenly felt that their horizons had been expanded, that a new light had been uncovered, that their senses had been heightened.

Slowly people learned which crystal stones could have the best effect on their spirit and soul; these were the round, natural crystal balls fashioned by nature.

People immediately associated the round shape of the stone with the sun, the source of life. It is easy, then, to understand why crystal was attributed with the properties of a god or a sun. People told themselves that if they carried the stone of the god or the sun, they themselves would have the strength of a god.

It is fascinating to see that this admiration of crystal balls is found in every culture and in every period. No culture has been found, for example, where people preferred simple pebbles to crystal balls.

The beliefs about crystal balls also explain why the rulers made sure to have some of these objects. The ruler felt that his authority and power were derived from the supreme god, as symbolized by the sun. The power of the crystal ball lay in its ability to transfer the authority of the supreme god to the ruler.

Alongside the development of the symbolic interpretation of crystal balls, their popular and mass use also increased, mainly for healing and soothsaying. The crystal ball was considered the easiest means of controlling the spirit or the mental force that develop prevision. We now know that crystals include a particular sequence of molecules that intensifies mental powers.

People who have a talent for fortune-telling and healing and a deep belief in the power of stones will be able to use crystal balls immediately, without any preparations, as a tool in their "work." Others will have to practice a little until they can put the properties of crystal to work in everyday life.

Round crystal balls are preferable to other shapes, unless the crystal is intended for a special purpose. A large crystal is preferable to a smaller one. However, the main factor determining the quality of the crystal ball is the clarity of the crystal. Perfect crystals, the size of a fist or larger and with maximum clarity, are valuable objects.

The first requirement when using a crystal ball is to enter a state of complete relaxation verging on meditation. In this state, take the ball in either or both hands and turn it slightly while focusing on the ball. As your vision is focused, you must also focus your thoughts inside the ball. Try to push your thoughts into the ball. In this state, you almost block out the body and its five senses, and act only on the level of the spirit, soul, and sixth sense. If you reach this stage, you will have succeeded in opening an astral channel between your innermost self and the crystal ball.

In this state, it is as if you become connected to a network of cables surrounding the whole world. The energy absorbed from the universe by the crystal ball starts to pass over to you. Suddenly you can see, hear, and know things that seem to be engraved on the crystal ball in invisible ink. Note that you see everything as if you were in the center of the ball looking out. **This is the right way to use a crystal ball.**

At this stage, you are now ready to concentrate your thoughts, "ask" questions, and receive answers. In fact, you are communicating with the universe past and present, through the means of the communication channel opened up for you by the crystal ball.

After completing your inner observation of the crystal ball, perform the whole process in reverse motion. Bring the lines of communication back inside yourself, and begin to operate again through your five senses and your body. Clean the crystal ball thoroughly using a piece of white cloth and put it in its storing place.

Sometimes, particularly in magic and black magic, crystal skulls are used. These are skulls carved from crystal and including quite accurate anatomical details. It is important to understand that the skull is of considerable importance in magic ceremonies. A person holding in his hand a skull-shaped crystal has a considerable impact on those who believe in his powers (we need only recall what Hamlet held in his hand in Shakespeare's play, and what it was that Faust looked up to).

Sometimes the skull is designed in a way that allows the jaw to be moved. By moving the "skull ball," the skull can talk to the believers (the magician hides behind a black screen). These skulls were very common in Catholic monasteries in the middle ages, and priests used to employ them to present spectacles, mainly for fundraising purposes. Some people even add eyes that can move in their sockets. The influence exerted by crystal skulls was so strong that the Church eventually forbade their use.

Another unique mystery is the type of skull known as Mitchell Hedges. These skulls are fashioned almost down to the last detail, without the skulls' bearing even a single mark showing the use of carving tools!

Much research has been carried out into these remarkable items. It has been claimed that they originate from other worlds and are part of entire "crystal people" who came to Earth thousands of generations ago, showing humans the way to a more advanced culture.

Crystal balls make a fascinating topic of discussion and are extensively used by clairvoyants — at every mystics fair there will be someone telling fortunes with a crystal ball. They are also widely used by healers. Nevertheless, it is important to remember that the crystal ball merely expands the uses and properties of "net" crystal.

Crystal can also be used to make pendulums, crosses, Stars of David, or charms, and can be integrated with other aspects of mysticism or with the use of jewels.

Crystals and the Use of the Pendulum

An ancient way to use crystals for healing and soothsaying is by means of a pendulum. In order to explain this method, a short description of the use of the pendulum, particularly for healing, is in order.

A pendulum comprises a small object with a center of gravity directed downward, attached to a strap of rope or leather (always of animal or vegetable origin, not synthetic). When the pendulum is held between the thumb and the index finger, the object moves into a vertical state. When the person holding the pendulum concentrates on a problem or question, the pendulum begins to sway. According to its movement, we can discern the answer to the question, engage in healing, or find missing objects.

(Another kind of pendulum is a twig or branch with a forked end, or a wire curved into a fork shape. This divining stick is used mainly for location — to search for water sources, quarries, or objects buried in the ground. You probably remember the Bible story of Moses striking the rock with a stick to draw forth water. Although the divining stick and the pendulum work according to the same principle — an object which concentrates the energy fluctuations of the person using it — we will relate here only to a pendulum and, to be specific, a pendulum where the "object" is made of crystal.)

From the above description, it will be clear that the person holding the pendulum, who effectively serves as its stand, must be the owner of the pendulum. A pendulum must be personal — the "person" may be the healer or user, not the patient or the person asking the question.

Crystals were used in pendulums as far back as ancient Babylon and Egypt. The preferred crystal for this purpose is quartz; the purer and clearer the quartz, the stronger the pendulum.

Of the different types of quartz, the most suitable are those known as single-point (single-terminated) or long quartz (pencil). These forms are most effective since they concentrate the gravity point downward according to the properties of crystal quartz.

However, this should in no sense be taken to imply that a pendulum cannot be made from another type of crystal or stone. In many cases the healer owns a large number of pendulums, each with a different stone or varying color and shape. The healer chooses the right color and shape of pendulum for the patient — a problem in the blood system will be addressed using a red ruby for example.

What we see here is essentially the application of the classification and colors of stones for healing to the field of medical pendulums.

It should be noted that the same cultures where crystals were used in pendulums also used them to make charms, personal seals, and jewelry. These, too, are examples of personal objects belonging to a specific individual, just as the healing pendulum belongs exclusively to the healer.

Once we have a pendulum in our hands, we can move on to understand the way it may be used. It is very easy to prepare a pendulum. All you need is a suitable crystal and a leather strap. Ready-made pendulums can be bought at any shop that sells crystals.

When you hold a pendulum, two types of movements may be found: circular movements (which may be partial or complete, clockwise or counter-clockwise) and straight movements, usually along a north-south axis.

As a preliminary stage, try holding the pendulum and distinguishing these different types of movement.

A pendulum essential serves to translate waves of inner energy emitted from the body holding the pendulum (although this information is external to the holder, residing in the patient or elsewhere, the flow of energy is from the outside to the person holding the pendulum, and then on to the pendulum itself).

After realizing that the pendulum indeed moves, try walking with it from place to place. You will soon discover that the environment has a dramatic impact on the pendulum (always remember that this is through the mediation of the person holding the pendulum).

This explains why effective use of the pendulum requires the neutralization of other factors emitting radiation or exerting an influence, such as the presence of other people or animals in the room, direct sunlight, metal objects, watches containing crystals, and so on.

A pendulum can only give three answers: **yes, no,** or **maybe.** "Maybe" means cases when it is impossible to tell whether the answer is yes or no. These are cases when the pendulum moves in straight lines and no circular movement can be detected. In any case when the pendulum moves in a straight line, there is no point trying to use the movement for soothsaying or healing.

Thus we are left with two answers: yes or no. This is a crucial point that is vital to appreciate. For example, we can hold a pendulum over the stomach of a person and ask a question (aloud or silently). After receiving the answer, we can ask another question, and so on. In each case, the answer will always be yes or no.

The following is a list of questions and answers during the healing process relating to a patient who complained of stomach pains. The healer holds the pendulum over the patient's bare stomach and asks the questions without directing them to the patient. The answer is given by the movement of the pendulum.

Question: Is this where the source of the pain lies?
Answer: Yes.
Question: Is it a tumor?

Answer: No.

Question: Is it an ulcer?

Answer: Yes.

Question: Is the ulcer due to a physical problem?

Answer: Maybe! (straight line!)

Question: Can the ulcer be cured using crystal-aided healing?

Answer: Yes...

And so on. At the end of the process, the healer held the pendulum over the heart chakra and asked that the stone might remove the feelings of tension and nervousness from the patient.

When we want to shorten the procedure or to try to receive answers to more complex questions, we may use aids such as an alphabet board or a diagram of the human body. We move the pendulum over the board and ask yes/no for each letter. Putting together the "yes" letters yields word or a name.

Similarly, the pendulum may be moved over a diagram of the human body. Yes/no questions are asked about illnesses.

Similar "continuous" questions are used when searching for something using the pendulum. Yet in each case the foundation is a simple yes/no question!

When the pendulum moves in a circular fashion, this may be expressed in two forms: clockwise or counter-clockwise. Each of these directions may mean either yes or no, and the direction may change for each healer, each pendulum, or each session.

In order to understand the language of the pendulum, we must "tune" the pendulum before beginning treatment. This is done as follows: take the pendulum and ask it a question the answer to which you know for certain. For example, ask "Am I reading a book now?" When a clockwise or counter-clockwise movement is received, it can be determined that this means "yes" for that person holding the pendulum for that particular pendulum, or for that point in time. The pendulum may now be used for the question we want to ask, and we will be able to interpret its movements.

If we take another pendulum, or the same one on a different day, we will have to "tune" it again and work out which direction means yes and which means no.

Since we are mainly concerned here with crystals used for healing, we may just mention briefly their use for soothsaying or predicting the future. In these cases, the pendulum is used by a soothsayer, usually a skilled medium, who uses the pendulum just as one might tarot cards or a crystal ball. However, the use of a crystal pendulum in healing is much more interesting phenomenon.

In this use, **the pendulum helps us**, as an initial stage, **to locate the place and cause of the disease through a long series of yes/no questions**.

It is here that the healer's skill in using the tool comes into play. The cardinal rule is for the healer to follow his or her feelings. By asking the patient questions without using the pendulum, we can locate the area that hurts and attempt to "guess" what might have caused the problem. Now we can take the pendulum, after "tuning," and start to ask questions and move forward step by step. It is important to appreciate that the goal here is to reach the energy field within the patient where the reason for the problem lies.

Suppose, for example, that we have managed to identify an energy field with an obstacle or problem that is causing the patient to suffer headaches. Will we be able to cure the headaches by healing?

Yes. This is the great advantage of the crystal pendulum over other types of pendulum. After identifying the problem and its origin, we must hold the crystal pendulum over the damaged energy field (or the problematic chakra).

Now the healer must concentrate his thoughts on sending positive, healing energies toward the patient. Research has proved that the unique structure of crystals causes a concentration of positive energy which is emitted from the end of the pendulum in the form of a concentrated spiral ray.

This ray of energy penetrates the surrounding energy (aura) of the patient, gently affecting the damaged area.

After treatment the pendulum should be cleaned in the same way as other crystal stones. It is advisable not to run more than one session a day, since the energy required on the part of the healer is enormous.

If a pendulum gives a large number of "maybe" answers (i.e., straight lines), and particularly if it is unable to decide on a yes/no "tuning" prior to beginning treatment, it should be given a chance to "rest" or even replaced.

A pendulum may also be used by an individual to treat themself. It is, of course, important to be familiar with the properties of crystal and of the pendulum. An individual who wishes to treat themself must have at least a basic knowledge of the principles of use of crystals, pendulums, and crystal healing.

When the patient takes on the role of healer, a high level of self-concentration is required. If successful, the healer-patient will be able to locate the source of the problem and help eliminate it, though this will take a long time (since the energy emitted from the person to the pendulum also includes damaged and negative energy). In these cases, purification prior to treatment is of the utmost importance. The individual must purify his body of negative energy as much as possible (including by use of purifying bathing), and use a strong, pure pendulum in an environment free of the influence of alien energies.

How do Crystals Grow?

When we look around us, we usually see only solid materials. Despite this, we are well aware that materials on Earth need not always be in solid form. There are also gasses such as oxygen and nitrogen, which comprise air and the entire atmosphere surrounding us; and, of course, there are liquids which indeed occupy most of the Earth's surface and are composed mainly of the hydrogen and oxygen that are the components of water. As humans, we live on the solid part of the Earth's surface, which explains why we are more aware of solid material than of the liquids on the planet.

The "solid" world of nature around us includes elements that are visibly alive — the animal and vegetable worlds — and the inanimate mineral kingdom. If, for example, we examine the composition of the animal and vegetable kingdoms, we will find that carbon is present in both in significant proportions. Yet in the mineral world, too, carbon is present in considerable quantities.

When addressing the mineral kingdom, we think mainly of rock. Although we can see mineral objects around us that are not rocks (mainly soil, sand and so on), it is important to recall that these are really no more than "rock fragments." In fact, most of the solid part of the Earth's surface is defined as solid rock. If we dig below this solid layer, we will reach the molten rock that is transformed into lava due to the intense temperatures of the Earth's inner core.

In the mineral world of rocks, too, we find substances that account for much of its bulk. Silicon, for example, accounts for almost one-third of the volume of the solid part of the Earth.

However, what is most eye-catching and appealing about the natural world is not the division into different elements, but the almost infinite variety of compounds created from a relatively small number of elements. Take insects, for example. There are tens of thousands of species of insects which differ from each other in shape, size, color, and so on. Yet if we "break down" these insects into elements such as hydrogen, carbon, oxygen, and so on, we will find no more than a few dozen elements!

This situation, which philosophers sometimes refer to as "diversity in unity," also applies to the mineral world.

Carbon, for example, is an element that forms both the most beautiful of diamonds and the blackest graphite in a pencil. One of these stones is precious and hard — the hardest stone of all. The other is the softest of all, dark and cheap.

Since our subject is crystals, which are a unique type of mineral compound, and precious stones, which represent no more than a drop in the ocean of rocks, we must understand that the stones we see in their raw or polished form on the shop counter are part of the world of nature that surrounds us. The thousands of different shapes of quartz crystal are all essentially compounds of one type of silicon or another, with various additions. In one place the element transforms into a diamond, while elsewhere it is manifested as graphite.

We shall attempt to understand the process by which crystals are created, and the powers crystals have by comparison to "ordinary" stones due to their process of creation, which imbues them with special properties.

Every mineral has different properties which dictate its physical behavior. Does the mineral **crack** or **split** into plates or cubes? In what way does it break? Can it be eroded? What sort of mark does burning leave on it? How hard is the mineral? What is its specific gravity? Can it be scratched? What effect does heat or cold have on it? Does it absorb water? And so on — a whole range of properties that eventually define the physical and chemical nature of the mineral.

As far as crystals are concerned, two additional properties are of importance for our purposes: the ability to transmit or fracture light rays, and the manner in which the crystal becomes charged with electricity when rubbed or pressed. These properties essentially dictate the type and value of the crystal, both in terms of price and rarity and in terms of the potential uses of its properties.

The main property of crystals as a mineral is that the

atoms form molecules and crystals which continue to grow according to a set sequence of sides which meet at set angles to form two- or three-pointed convergence points.

During this pre-determined and fixed process of crystallization, the crystal is divided into definable parts. Each symmetrical part matches another part, and any given part will always be the symmetrical image of another one.

Moreover, in examining the axes that pass through the crystal structure, we can classify the various forms in terms of mineralogical research and classification into meaningful shapes: a cube, an octahedron (eight equilateral triangles — characteristic of diamonds), hexahedron (six squares), dodecahedron (twelve rhombuses — characteristic of the garnet family). A triangular octahedron, where each surface on the octahedron forms a pyramid, is characteristic of perfect diamonds. Other forms are also found — six-times octahedrons, four-times cubes, deltoids, and so on.

What is important to understand here is not the precise and complex form in which crystals are found, but the fact that perfect laws define these shapes.

Do these perfect laws limit the variety of crystals or the range of diversity in unity?

No. The reason is that extraordinarily complex crystals can be found: crystals which are part cube and part octahedron, or where one part has double sides and one triple sides.

The crystals we use are actually composed of an enormous number of small crystals, sometimes differing from each other, which develop inside and next to one another. Only rarely do we find a crystal that is all built according to a single pattern.

It should also be stressed that although most of the solid material on Earth is found in one type of crystal or another, we are interested here only in crystals that have developed to significant proportions, not in infinitesimal particles of matter. A pea-sized diamond is large and valuable, yet emeralds may be as large as a human and weigh hundreds of kilograms. We mine diamonds and emeralds and ignore all the surrounding waste material, though this, too, contains innumerable tiny crystals.

We have referred here to a "growing" or "developing" crystal as if crystals were living things. Can we really attribute the property of growth to inanimate crystals?

Rock, as understood in everyday terms, may be created in a number of ways. It may be crystallized particle after particle around a nucleus of some kind; it may be created as the result of an eruption or rift (lava erupting from inside the Earth cools to form basalt); it may be created as the result of the death of a creature or plant, as in the case of coral or fossils.

When we talk of crystallization, we refer to a process that all of us recognize, but few of us have stopped to consider. The process of crystallization may be compared to what happens if we place a magnet on a board and then sprinkle iron dust around the magnet. The dust will be drawn to the magnet — first the closer particles, creating a symmetrical form with its own laws around the magnet. After the first particles have been magnetized, they accumulate power and subsequently attract the more distant particles to join the structure around the magnet.

Another example is a block of ice placed in water below 0° Celsius. The water will start to turn to ice — first around the ice, and later across the entire surface.

This is the process of crystallization. A nucleus (the magnet or block of ice in our examples) begins the entire process, and structures crystallize around it in a fixed form. This process only **strengthens the crystal, and does not sap its energies!**

When a stream of lava spurts out of a volcano, the further the stream of lava flows from the mouth of the volcano, the weaker it becomes. Its heat decreases and it moves more slowly, until it eventually solidifies into rock. Yet the bigger crystal grows and the further its edges are from the nucleus, the stronger and more powerful it becomes.

This property is characteristic of living things. A sperm joins with an ovum, one cell splits into two... four... eight, into a fetus, new-born baby, child and adult. Most crystals grow in precisely the same way.

It is important to appreciate that the growth process of

the crystal is actually timeless. When we examine the creation of crystals, we bring our own concepts of time, but the crystal has its own laws defining time, even if we can also use our own familiar concepts.

Some crystals take hundreds of thousands of years to develop (no, this is not a typing error!) A crystal celebrating its 500,000th birthday is nothing exceptional. In Russia there is a beryl crystal block weighing almost two tons; it has been estimated that this block is almost 800,000 years old. Even quite small quartz crystals may have an age of 100,000 years or more in human terms. Note that we are talking only about the period in which the crystal continues to grow, live, and crystallize! A quartz aged 100,000 years and still in its natural environment (i.e., with free "quartz" atoms around it that can join on) will have a different and larger form when it reaches the age of 200,000.

Other crystals, as the result of sudden change (a blow of some kind) engendering tremendous pressure, extreme heat, a particular chemical environment, etc., pass through their entire growth period in a single "leap" and then stop developing. Diamonds, for example, reach a final state at which they stop crystallizing. Plaster crystals are created within a few hours and then stop growing. Here the growing time of the crystal has been "squashed" into a tiny fraction of time from our perspective, due to an external force, but the strength of the crystalline time compensates for this.

Thus external factors, usually extreme, influence the

growing time of a crystal, just as enzymes can be used to accelerate the growth of plants or animals.

It is worth mentioning another means by which crystals are formed: a material is present in liquid or steam form, and particular elements in the material evaporate or disintegrate, resulting in the crystal's emergence in a pure form. Although this process differs from the normal growth process of crystals, it is actually no more than a mirror image of the normal process — the growth is inward, and the crystal is yielded by the material as a whole.

Once we understand how crystals or precious stones are formed, we can appreciate the tremendous force of a crystal, and why it contains an infinite amount of energy.

Imagine a cinema camera placed in some location one hundred thousand years ago, and recording its impressions year after year right down to the present day. Just think how much information the lens would have recorded.

This is exactly what the crystal is. It absorbs energy year after year, and any energy it absorbs brings in "impressions" from the outside world. It is a living body that accumulates powers, stores energy, and does not need to emit energy in order to continue to live, unlike humans, animals or plants.

When we remove a crystal from under the ground, or find one in a natural setting, it usually contains all the treasures of energy it has accumulated over hundreds of thousands of years. The bigger the crystal, the stronger the energy it contains.

When we refer to energy, we are using a term drawn from the field of human science. But the energy in crystals differs from the usual sense of the word — it is electromagnetic energy, which we do not yet know quite how to measure or to use to the maximum to benefit humanity.

Cortés, the Spaniard who conquered and subjugated Latino America, found that the natives of Mexico kept a stone we now identify as emerald in their homes and worshipped it as if it were a god. He collected several hundred beautiful stones of this type in a crate weighing four hundred kilograms to take them back to the King of Spain. While traveling from America to Spain, his ship ran into a storm that threatened to capsize the ship (in the region now known as the Bermuda Triangle).

"The ship sailing alongside us burst into flame like a straw when hit by the lightening, despite the torrential rain that was falling. Under the black clouds I saw the ship hit again and again by lightening until it was carried off and vanished from sight. The wall of lightening seemed like fire descending from the heavens, drawing ever nearer to my ship... Even the toughest of my sailors saw their death before them and quickly kissed the cross... Then, God heard the prayer of my heart, and the wall of lightening stopped short of the ship, creating a dome of fire over the ship and its surroundings... It was God's will that my ship might be saved."

Two hundred years later, Matoleamos, a researcher into precious stones, wrote in his book: "And the property of the stone called emerald, brought from Rio Minoro [a famous mine in Colombia active to this day], is its capacity to provide powerful protection against lightening or fire, since the power in it repulses the power of fire and lightening. **It was Cortés's luck that he brought with him this stone, which saved him and his ship..."**

Even in the present New Age, we are still not aware of the full strength and force of crystals. They hide more than they have revealed, and occasionally we uncover another fraction of their extraordinary power. If we wish to understand their magic charm and strength, we must recall that crystals are part of nature, governed by its laws — the same laws that guide our own lives and those of every creature on Earth and in the universe.

The Legacy of Crystals

When archaeologists uncovered the tomb of the Egyptian pharaoh Tutankhamen within the pyramid, it was considered the archaeological find of the century. Many sections of the tomb had been preserved intact, and the discovery greatly expanded our knowledge of ancient Egypt.

Within a few years, however, many of the members of the delegation were struck down by a mysterious and unknown disease that came to be known as the "disease of the pharaohs." At first, the disease was attributed to a mysterious bacteria preserved in the sealed tomb. However, later examinations of the explorers uncovered additional information: a single-pointed, obelisk-like crystal with a number of hieroglyphic signs engraved on the base.

Was this crystal a seal or guard for the pharaoh's tomb? Did its curse strike anyone who invaded the sanctity of the tomb?

In the Great Mongolian desert, on the present-day border between China and Mongolia, the landscape undergoes frequent changes. One year, a wide river flows through a sandy channel, yet next year there is nothing but sand. These frequent changes are caused by the strong winds in the region, and by the fact that most of the desert is made up of shifting sands. These sands instantaneously uncover and hide ancient cities.

In 1984 an ancient Chinese border fort was suddenly and unexpectedly revealed. The fort had been preserved almost in its entirety underneath the sand. Large expeditions of Chinese archaeologists arrived at the site, and under a cloak of secrecy began to investigate the fortress. The excavations uncovered a hidden corridor leading to a deep cellar. When the researchers opened the great stone door blocking the entrance to the cellar, they were astonished by what they found.

The cellar contained a real treasure trove which has already become a legend: a collection of jade statues of one of the emperors of ancient China. This priceless collection was arranged on shelves, and the statues were free of any dust, showing just how well the cellar had been sealed from the desert sands.

The Chinese archaeologists quickly removed the statues and took them to a secret location in China. In China, archaeological excavations are considered no less a state secret than military research. This time, though, the discovery "exploded" loudly after seventy-three members of the expedition died of a mysterious and unknown disease three weeks after the cellar was opened!

The Chinese were at least aware of the source of the disease. They called it "the curse of the stone," and placed the blame on a large, translucent piece of crystal shaped like a cylinder found in the treasure cellar.

These two stories illustrate the capacity of crystals to transmit "curses" or "blessings." Crystal is a material that can be charged. By the time it reaches the "end user," the stone already carries a significant load, from the quarrier or explorer who found it, through the polisher, salesperson, and so on. However, these influences are slight and may be easily cleansed from the stone.

The situation is very different when the stone has been charged deliberately with a considerable strength through engraving. In such cases, the crystal carries a strong concentration of positive or negative energy that may continue to exert an influence even after many generations.

For the crystal or stone, the passage of time is meaningless. Time is not a factor in the life of the stone. The moment a person activates a stone — takes it in his hands or invades its space — the stone will begin to emit or radiate its charge, which may have been acquired the day before or thousands of years ago. It is as if we were to take a tape recorder and turn it on, immediately hearing whatever was recorded the day before, or a year ago, or a very long time ago...

When crystal is "activated," the radiation it emits transmits the message stored in the stone. It is important to realize that this radiation or message require a "key" in order to be absorbed. Not everyone who approaches an uncovered stone will be harmed if the stone carries a curse. However, since the stone was meant to transmit in a general sense, rather than to a specific individual, the range of reception will be broad and wide, encompassing quite a large number of people.

If a stone is meant to help women become pregnant, its range of action will be limited to women of a particular age who wish to become pregnant and are having difficulties doing so. If we want to guard a tomb, the range of the "charge" must be much greater. This explains why some people were harmed at the pharaoh's tomb in Egypt or the cellar of treasures in China, while others escaped harm.

The closer a person is to the culture from which the crystal came, the more likely it is that they will be exposed to the curse of the stone (or its blessing). An archaeologist investigating China or Egypt will probably be exposed to these ancient cultures. The more removed someone is from knowledge of, or belief in, the culture from which the stone comes, the more protected they will be.

We may understand this in another way. Every crystal that has been used by humans has its own legacy, the accumulation of radiation that has passed through it. Unrefined stone carries the most basic, existential, or primal legacy. A normal stone carries an accumulated legacy encompassing a "horizontal" range of cultures and people. A stone that has been used for a particular purpose carries an accumulated "vertical" legacy in a particular field and with a much greater intensity.

Since each person, and actually each being, has an enormous unknown sphere of the subconscious, of accumulated collective memory (of an entire culture or universe) and individual memory (from previous incarnations), the exposure of the crystal to this subconscious pool creates a wide range of contacts. The quantity and force of these contacts varies from person to person and from stone to stone. It is these contacts that represent the influence of the stone's legacy on that particular person.

In other words, crystals are a trigger or key to releasing the individual's subconscious. We are aware mainly of the conscious, of human memory, of the knowledge and information we see in front of our eyes. Stones carry and reveal another pool of memory, knowledge, and information inside us that operates on the subconscious level. The interaction between the subconscious legacy of the individual and the legacy of the stone opens up new worlds to those who use crystals wisely.

One last comment: we began this section with a description of the "curse of the crystal," which is a well-known phenomenon. It is important to stress, however, that in most cases crystals carry a neutral legacy, that was not deliberately charged with either good or evil intent, or a blessing legacy, since most stones were used to bring good, rather than to curse or to punish.

Purifying Crystals

The concept of purifying crystals relates to an action designed to restore the stone to its original, primal nature, as it was before it began to absorb the influence of alien frequencies. We must remember that just as we receive frequencies from the stone, so it receives frequencies from us and from its surroundings.

Opinions are divided as to the need to purify stones. Some people claim that we must purify the stone to the best of our ability and restore it to its original state. Others argue that everything the stone has accumulated to date is the "experience" of the past and defines the character of the stone. Just as we would not erase the "experience" of a human, neither should we delete the stone's experience. **Note that we are not talking here about negative residues that must be removed during cleaning, for a stone as for a human!**

We shall describe here the method for purifying stones, along with a simple word of advice: do what you feel you should do! If you feel that the stone you chose needs to be purified — go ahead! That's all there is to it.

To purify a crystal, take a tablespoonful of salt,

preferably coarse sea salt, and put it in a cup of water. If you use sea water, add half a teaspoonful of salt to the cup. Then soak the crystal in the saltwater overnight.

(There is a theory that the saltwater "seals" the stone and prevent energy radiation being emitted. However, we favor the approach that argues that saltwater has the property of conducting energy more effectively than ordinary water. Accordingly, the saltwater "attracts" the energy we wish to extract from the stone.)

In the morning, remove the stone from the cup and wash it in running water. Before washing, feel the stone. If it is warm, it should be washed in lukewarm rather than cold water. Dry the stone and leave it to "rest" during the day before using it.

This process of purification can be used not only for a new stone we have just bought that we wish to restore to its "virgin" state, but also for stones we own that have been exposed to strong and concentrated use, such as for the purposes of meditation, promoting pregnancy, or an astral journey. In these cases, too, purifying the stone restores it to its original state.

Other methods of purifying stones can also be found, including placing the stone in a cup of water under the moonlight for a night; or burying it in moist soil for three days. Another method, used mainly for stones already in use, is to dry the stone with a soft cloth, using circular movements. When drying a stone in this way, it is important to treat the stone as if it were an adored baby, and to think only positive thoughts.

The saltwater method is the most effective, particularly in the case of a new stone and a person without experience with crystals.

A higher level of purification is through imagery. Imagine waves or waterfalls repeatedly washing over the stone. If the individual is aware of themself and capable of focusing their imagery in the desired direction, this method will be just as effective as actually washing the crystal in saltwater.

The Use of Stones in Healing

In order to understand the blessing of crystals and prepare ourselves physically and mentally to receive this blessing, we must understand the principles of healing which explain the way the stone works.

For this purpose, we may see every stone, and particularly a crystal, as an antenna that receives and transmits frequencies or energy. What is special about this antenna is that it sifts and analyzes these frequencies before deciding which to transmit on. Moreover, the stone usually intensifies and strengthens its own special energy frequency or wave.

A trained person — healer or patient — holds the stone in his hand and transmits a particular form of energy radiation **to the stone**. Depending on its properties and the intention implanted and structured in it, the stone receives this energy, intensifies it, and transmits a stronger and more unique energy frequency more appropriate to the healer's intentions.

Anyone who knows a little about photography will recognize this process without difficulty. By placing a particular filter over the lens, the camera suddenly absorbs a particular color, and the photograph may be devoid of the color red or blue, or, depending on the filter, anything green will appear to be red, and so on.

Stones work in a similar way. We transmit radiation to them, together with our intention to a specific goal. The stone receives this intention, sifts and intensifies the energy, and emits a strong energy wave to the patient. This wave acts on what is known as electro-magnetic energy, repairing the aura at its weak points according to the healer's intentions. A number of characteristics of this process must be understood:

* There must be a correlation between the type of stone used and the imbalance or problem we wish to solve.

* The person operating the stone is a "trigger" or "spark" and provides the intention directed to the stone.

* A stone can only mend something that is present in a person's body, spirit, or soul. For example, if someone has no spark of sexual energy, all the stones in the world will not be able to provide this person with sexual energy. The property of the stone or, more precisely, the property of the energy sent from the person to the stone, is to balance and strengthen electro-magnetic energy. But this happens by nurturing an energetic seed that must be present in the individual. If no such energetic seed — however tiny — is present, the stone will be useless.

(We might add that this is precisely the property of crystals themselves: without a "seed" or nucleus from which the crystal may develop, it will never crystallize.)

If we remember these "rules," we will be aware of the properties and limitations of stones as an aid in healing in the widest sense.

We shall also add here a number of general comments relating to the use of stones for physical and spiritual healing, particularly concerning the right way to use stones according to an understanding of the basis of the spiritual relationship between the stone and the human who draws on the stone's blessing:

   * Every stone has its own special energy radiation. If we do not know exactly what the property of the stone is, the energy may be determined according to its color. There are five basic energy colors: white, red, blue, yellow, and green. Charging a stone increases its color energy property, while transmiting or emptying the stone reduces its color property.

   * When a stone transmits, its color property is intensified. After treatment, the stone is "empty" and has a shortage of its unique color energy property.

   * Every stone has a surrounding "aura" according to its shape. This aura comes into contact with the aura of the

healer and/or patient. If the stone's aura is incompatible with that of the patient, some form of "disconnection" will ensue.

* Patients sometimes isolate themselves with black or brown auras. In such cases, there is almost no chance that the stone's energy will be able to radiate successfully to the patient.

* When a stone is charged to its maximum capacity, it indicates this to us through hot or cold waves or by a prickly sensation on our skin.

* A stone should not be charged beyond its capacity.

* Green energy is the most effective for charging stones and is the most powerful form.

* Yellow energy may lead to a sense of apathy on the part of the patient, or to spiritual "anesthesia."

* Blue radiation may cause muscle tension and a hardening sensation on the skin.

* Red radiation may cause overheating in the body and blood problems.

* Stones indicate their charge state through heat or

cold. It is important to learn to feel the stone and sense its state.

* Every stone has a positive pole and a negative pole. The stone must be held correctly for transmiting or receiving.

* The stone should be held no more than an arm's length from the patient. At greater distances, it is difficult for us to focus the stone's radiation on the damaged area, or on the chakras we wish to influence.

* The radiation from different stones mingles and pollutes. It is important to keep stones separately and to divide one stone from another. In treatment, the healer should undergo bathing and purification when moving from one stone to another, unless the intention is to blend different radiations.

* After treatment, the stone is empty and must be allowed to rest.

Healng and Crystals

The use of crystals in healing is well known to those who are familiar with crystals, as well as to healers, physicians, fortune-tellers, and innumerable patients.

These wonderful stones can be used to adjust blood pressure, heal wounds, join broken bones, ease pain and migraines, and sometimes even to alleviate and cure diseases that are considered terminal.

The internal structure of crystals is the most perfect of any in the mineral world. The internal balance reflects the balance found on the border between inanimate and animate; and, as we know, on the borders between one state and another, an enormous amount of energy is accumulated. This energy can be found in crystals and, if properly used, can heal us.

The more perfect a crystal, and the more we succeed in choosing the right stone for the person's needs (of body, spirit, and soul), the better the energy flow will be. The crystal will absorb negative energy from the sick person and charge them with positive and healing energy.

Crystal provides us with powerful, concentrated energy that may be transferred — all we need to do is learn to use it properly!

We know that injury to an individual's astral body,

soul, or spirit is invariably expressed in injury to the physical body. We also know that the astral body is essentially a concentration of different energies. Accordingly, the best tool for treating a radiation-based and energy-based body is crystal, with its concentrated energy.

A trained healer uses a crystal as if it were a spiritual "scalpel" — repairing energy fields, removing purulent energy, and thus healing the patient. The better the relationship between healer, patient, and crystal, the easier this task will be.

Even when an individual uses a crystal on his own, the most important thing is the relationship created between him or her and the stone.

Crystals are the most sophisticated natural scalpels. Scientists have found that if the human body had as perfect a structure as that of crystals, we would all be like children of the gods, with extraordinary and wonderful capabilities. However, it appears that during the transition from crystal to living bodies, something went wrong in our bodies' systems; and no one is more aware than each one of us of our own imperfections!

In order to exploit the positive energy in crystals, the individual (healer or patient) must reach a state where they transmit on the same "wavelength" as the crystal. Every stone has its own energy rhythm, just as every person has his own energy rhythm; only when the two are coordinated can energy pass from the person to the stone and vice versa. In other words, what we must achieve is harmony.

When harmony prevails between crystals and humans, problems may be solved.

When a healer uses a crystal, the goal is not to draw energy from the crystal. On the contrary, the healer charges the crystal with positive, loving energy which is intensified by the crystal and then sent to the patient's body. The healer attempts to direct the energy beam to the weak point in the patient's energy body.

It is important, therefore, to be familiar with the chakras and the systems surrounding each chakra. The chakra serves as a kind of gate through which energy may be inserted; from these points, the energy will be disseminated along all the "roads" connected to that chakra.

Crystals are sometimes portrayed as a powerful energy amplifier, which is indeed how they are used in various physical and mechanical appliances. Crystals can turn a little loving energy into a lot of healing energy.

This loving energy may then be passed on to the patient, or the patient may even pass it on to himself, using various means: hugging, a pleasant word, meditation, prayer... Whatever the means, though, it must be concentrated — only a crystal can take an energy flow and amplify it one hundred times or more!

Think of sun rays. They provide warmth and light, but they cannot start a fire. Yet if we take a lens (or a suitable crystal) and concentrate the sun's rays, we obtain a powerful ray that can light a fire.

This is precisely the use that healers make of crystals.

When we use the sun and a lens to light a fire, any clouding or shadow on the lens will prevent us from succeeding. The same is true of crystals. In order to use crystals as efficiently as possible, we must cleanse our thoughts and spirit of anything that might cast a shadow over the crystal. A healthy and clean soul leads to a healthy body! This is why the process of cleaning and relaxation or meditation before using crystals is so important.

There are many methods for using and activating crystals; everyone chooses the method they prefer according to their experience and inclination. The only advice we can give to those seeking a method is to choose the one that will be most effective for you! Although personal choice is not always rational, it is the best way.

Some place a "love-charged" crystal on the body, while others hold the crystal above the damaged chakra. Some move the crystal over the chakra (cleaning away the negative energy every so often), while others leave the stone motionless for a long period. Any method may be used, as long as it is in the patient's best interests.

It is important to understand that the relationship between humans and crystals may only be described (given our limited terms) as one of imagery.

In other words, if we feel intense heat or inflammation, we will hold the crystal (preferably on the "heart's side," i.e., in our left hand) and attempt to maximize "cool" energy, by thinking of cold.

When we wish to repair an energy hole in the base chakra, for example, we should think of the functions of this system — life, sex, etc. — and use imagery to direct energy. If we wish to repair the green aura of the astral body, we should think of the color green or a green landscape, thus drawing the green energy from within the crystal.

Guided imagery works as a "trigger" to activate the crystal and yield benefits for humans!

Some people think of crystals as "magic stones," because they are unaware of the inter-relationship between the stone and the human consciousness. Despite this, a subconscious process of imagery occurs without the person's being aware of this, so that the crystal can still fulfill its function.

It should be recalled that crystals, like magnets, have a positive energy pole and a negative energy pole. An acquaintance with the personal crystal of the healer or patient will enable us to determine the right way to hold or place the crystal.

The basic rule is that the left-hand side of the patient draws positive energy from the positive side of the crystal, while the right-hand side of the patient releases negative energy to the negative side of the crystal. Accordingly, the crystal should be shaken every now and then, with the negative pole held away from us, in order to "brush off" and remove the negative energy.

If we are not sure of the precise way to use the crystal, but nevertheless wish to use it to ease pain, for example, the best advice is to hold the crystal in our left hand opposite the source of pain, with the stone held between the thumb and index finger, and then roll the stone as if it were a prayer bead. This will enable you to feel the right way to hold the crystal.

The size of the crystal used for healing is an important factor. The stone must sit comfortably in the holder's palm. The "feeling" the stone gives in the hand is extremely significant. In addition, and despite the fact that the most important factor is the clarity of the crystal, size is important. The crystal serves to amplify the human consciousness, and we sometimes need a stronger amplifier in order to get good results.

Crystals are often used by healers who employ Eastern practices such as acupuncture and massage. Pointed crystals may be used instead of acupuncture needles, with one important difference: **the crystal is never used to puncture the skin, but merely to press against it!** In this way, a crystal may be used for local healing of a blockage in the Chi or energy flow by controlled pressing.

This process takes place by identifying the blockage in the patient's Chi and placing the crystal at this point, with the positive end pointing down. The crystal is held in the left hand. Crystal treatment usually takes place at a distance of approximately five centimeters from the body. In this case, however, we press the skin lightly and continue to press until we sense that the blockage has been released.

The second method is through a general or local massage. For this purpose, we use round or cylindrical crystals which are moved over the aching area in massaging movements. It is important to "shake" the crystal from time to time and to use short, repetitive movements when massaging, without allowing the crystal to remain on any one spot on the body for too long. It is important to notice the patient's reactions, particularly since using a stone to massage someone may be painful.

Crystal is a good tool for receiving feedback, and the sense of pain or relief on the part of the patient will be sensed immediately by the healer. Experience and knowledge are essential for this type of use.

It should be appreciated that to some extent crystals "invite" people to exchange energies with them. This is why the healer holds the stone in his left hand and "waves" it over the patient's body, thus hinting to the body which route may be used to exchange energies.

However, contact is not always made between the stone and the patient's energy body. If the right channel of communication cannot be found, the patient's body should be gently "brushed" with the stone. This will open new paths to reach the chakras or the energy field.

It must be emphasized that, like any other type of healing, crystal healing requires a good rapport between healer and patient, or between the patient and themself in the case of self-treatment.

Since the system in which crystals work is parallel to the self-imagery system of the individual, we must help the stone by imagining the treatment or thinking about the method of treatment. When looking for an opening to transfer energy, for example, we must think, or even say aloud, "Open before me the energy opening of the heart chakra!" Successful crystal healing usually depends on inner devotion or imagery on the part of those involved.

Color, Healing and Crystals

Crystal healing — one of the commonest uses of crystals — is intimately related to the colors of the stone. Moreover, we know that colors have the capacity to heal on their own. When we combine the healing power of stones with that of colors, we obtain a powerful healing tool.

Color is an extremely important factor in human life. The first divisions between humans were based on differences of skin color, second only to the distinction between men and women.

Color is an important part of the way we relate to our environment. In a simple experiment carried out in Cambridge, 300 students of similar academic abilities took examinations in two large halls. The first hall was painted red, and the second one was blue. Which group got the better results? Intuitively, you will choose the blue group, and that is quite true. What is surprising is the difference in the average grades — 22%. There can be no doubt that most of this difference is due to the color of the halls.

Each color affects us differently or activates different properties, abilities, and reactions in us. Fashion designers are well aware of this; cinematographers use color and reactions to color extensively; and painters have researched and studied the mysteries of color.

When we wish to arouse "healing" responses in our body and soul, in order to overcome a particular disease or the cause of disease, we can use colors to create that reaction. The specific color wave we receive creates a given reaction, just as in more "conventional" medical treatment.

The world of nature around us provides us with an extensive and varied laboratory in which to learn about the use of color in nature, the properties of different colors, and their healing powers. All we need to do is to observe nature and learn.

Sometimes when I take my dog out for a walk, he approaches some grass or plants and eats it. Grass is not a normal food for him, but eating it cleanses his intestines. Could there be a connection between the green color of grass and the "medical treatment" my dog gives himself?

When walking in nature — the natural setting of colors — we may distinguish the effect of colors on our physical and, in particular, our emotional health. We can examine this just by asking ourselves simple questions.

For example, let us take five mood states that we all know cause physical reactions: **stress, anxiety, calm, depression,** and **self-confidence.** Now try to imagine yourself in a natural environment in which there is color, and try to feel what mood would be aroused in each of the following settings:

1. On a mountain top in the middle of the desert, surrounded by **yellow** and heat.

2. On the seashore facing the **red** setting sun against the backdrop of the **blue** sea and the **yellow** beach.

3. In a field of nothing but **green**, the green grass blowing gently in the breeze.

4. In a plowed field of **brown** furrows.

And so on.

You will soon discover that particular colors have their own characteristics that may accelerate or slow down physical and mental processes — in other words, they affect the healing of the body!

It must be remembered that different cultures attach different significance to colors in general and, in many cases, to the specific properties of each color. The association of blue with the treacherous sea means that it creates a feeling of insecurity in some cultures, while in others — for the same reason — it may inspire confidence and daring. White may symbolize either mourning or joy. Yellow may mean sickness or health; and so on. We must not overlook the connection between color and culture.

In broad terms, the different "color cultures" may be divided into four groups: the Far East; the tropical cultures; western culture (mainly European and American); and the northern cultures, including those countries dominated by ice and with extreme changes in the relative length of night and day. Some colors evoke identical responses in all color cultures, but the differences should be born in mind, particularly those between the western color culture and that of the east.

Since color is also an important factor in crystals, the response to an identical crystal may differ from one culture to another.

Our description of the meanings of color is based on the western color culture. Where this differs from other cultures, we will emphasize this point.

As we all know, the term "body" refers to a number of overlapping and integrated systems: the physical body, the ethereal body, the emotional body, and so on. We can see and feel our physical body, and we can see and recognize our aura — the energy "envelope" that surrounds our physical body. **The influence of color, whether benign or malign, passes exclusively though the aura or the "mental" body, from which point the influence extends to the physical body**. In other words, the use of color in healing physical problems and faults involves an indirect influence via a mediator, **just as in the use of crystals and stones**.

Various healers, particularly those who use crystals, have been involved in "color healing" for many years. Over this time, they have studied the properties of different colors and allocated spheres to each color.

This approach is usually based on the colors of the rainbow (which are also the most common colors in nature). The seven colors of the rainbow may be divided among the seven chakras according to a parallel system: **red corresponds to the base chakra, while violet or purple (at the other end of the rainbow) corresponds to the crown chakra**. The division of the chakras continues in this manner across the colors of the rainbow.

We shall now detail in brief the properties of the various colors in terms of the use of crystals in healing. As already mentioned, we will emphasize the prevailing approaches in the cultures of the west, where we live, and in the east, which has greatly influenced attitudes to healing and crystals in the west.

Red

The color red is used to treat problems relating to the blood system (anemia, high or low blood pressure, insufficient oxygen in the blood, or "lack of vitality"). The color red strengthens the body but also increases nervous tension; accordingly, excessive use may be unwise, if negative symptoms are to be prevented.

The use of red stones is concentrated and requires extreme caution. Correct use may strengthen and empower the body.

Special and cautious use of red has served to increase sexual desire and to treat sexual problems relating to a lack of sufficient sexual energy. This is why red is considered to be the color of love.

Orange

The color orange is used to treat problems involving the lungs and various glands. Particularly effective in treating muscle cramps. Used to treat respiratory problems (asthma). A special use is for women during their menstrual period. The color orange adds "zest" to the physical body.

Bear in mind that excessive or erroneous use of the color orange leads to aggression, detachment from the environment, and, above all, to an imbalance between the individual and the environment (leading to feelings of inferiority or superiority).

Orange is useful mainly for securing self-confidence, for realizing intellectual capacities, and for maintaining the verve or drive needed to make the most of human capabilities in any sphere.

Yellow

Yellow is used mainly in treating the digestive system, and is particularly effective for dietary problems. It is important to appreciate that in healing, the digestive system includes not only the digestive organs used to process food, but also the organs and processes used to take nutrition to all parts of the body or to remove it, as, for example, through the skin. Thus the color yellow influences the entire body, although, as stated, it is mainly used for the functions of digestion, distribution, and excretion.

Yellow is also a "fuel" for the nervous system. A surfeit of yellow "floods" the system, impairing bodily functions, particularly in terms of resistance. The main function of yellow, when properly used, is to enhance the sense of well-being and the ability to cope effectively and cheerfully with everyday life.

Green

Green is used mainly to treat the heart, including problems of the blood system, for pressures in the head (headaches and migraines), and for cell growth problems (including malignancy problems).

However, the main use of green reflects the fact that this is the balancing color, located precisely in the middle of the rainbow. Accordingly, its main property is to promote balance in physical and mental systems.

It is difficult to use too much green in treatment, but if this happens, the person feels as if he is "eating himself from inside." The proper and effective use of green is mainly for strengthening, overcoming obstacles, and opening new paths.

If you do not know which color or stone to use for a given problem, the best advice is to use a green stone (cautiously) until you discover what the problem is and can decide on a more precise solution.

Blue

The color blue is used for respiratory and inflammatory problems. The main property of blue is to promote calmness and tranquility, or coolness, in the body.

This is a calming color that builds bridges between the world of the physical body and the world of the mental and spiritual body.

Excessive or incorrect use of blue may lead to "coolness" of the soul — anxiety, depression, or pathological apathy. Proper use will lead mainly to the positive integration of the individual in his environment and society.

Indigo

This is a deep blue/violet color used to treat problems relating to both the upper chakras — sight, hearing, smell, and the entire nervous system. Indigo is also effective in treating mental imbalances.

Indigo seems to "open up" humans to positive influences in their environment, and this is why it is so important.

This color should be used carefully, since too much indigo causes grave problems, particularly in terms of behavioral changes due to an excessively "charged" nervous system. Proper and skilled use, by contrast, will promote balance, integration, and inspiration on a high level.

Some people also use indigo to treat an excess of other colors, as if it were a kind of "color antidote." This should only be attempted by expert healers.

Violet (or Purple)

A special color used to treat the nervous system and

the patient's mental body. However, violet is also used to purify the blood system and regulate the metabolic and cellular activity of the body. Extreme caution is required in using this color. Excessive or incorrect use of violet will cause nervous imbalance and phenomena such as epilepsy, fainting, or severe dizziness.

Violet is the uppermost color we can use to treat humans with the level of knowledge we currently possess. Enlightenment, training, or higher consciousness all require some form of usage of the color violet.

If we recall the color principles outlined above, we may take a given crystal and **use it according to the color of the stone**.

In transmitting a particular color to the body requiring treatment, the use of a stone whose color matches the one we are transmitting increases the potency of the treatment enormously. We could, for example, treat the aura with the color green by walking through a green field. But while this would have some effect, the use of a green crystal to transmit healing green energy to the body will be much more powerful and concentrated than the walk in a field.

There is an argument as to whether the strong influence of crystal is due to its color waves or to the concentrated electro-magnetic energy it contains. For healing purposes, this is not really important. Both these properties of crystal are put to use when we engage in crystal healing.

Different stones, and even different examples of the same group or type of stone, differ in terms of their ability to assist in color healing. The basic rule is that the bigger the stone and the cleaner and clearer its color, the greater its influence. Accordingly, crystal including two colors is not effective for color healing. We must search for crystals with a clearly defined color and with the maximum possible clarity.

One last comment. The most effective use of colored crystals in healing comes when both the healer and the patient are in a state of imagery matching the stone color. This use of imagery in crystal healing is complex and involved. Here, however, we should explain to readers the nature of imagery during treatment.

Suppose that a healer chooses a green stone. He will then concentrate his thought on the stone in order to send a green energy beam to the patient. This is the standard and essential treatment.

The idea of imagery is that if the healer, during treatment, is in a state in which he is imagining himself in a green environment, for example in a field, the influence of the energy beam will be much greater. And the effect will be even greater still if the patient, too, imagines themself to be in a green environment. The maximum possible effect is obtained during treatment when healer and patient both imagine themselves to be in an appropriate color setting for the color of stone used in the treatment.

Chakras and Crystals

A key concept in crystals, healing, and auras is the chakra. We shall try to understand this concept and the philosophy it reflects, and to appreciate how these may be used.

As we know, in and around the human body there is an invisible energy field responsible for operating the physical and mental systems of each individual. Within this field there are concentrations or centers of energy which stand out both in terms of the concentration of energy they contain, and by their function as "junctions" for specific energy networks.

If we imagine the energy fields and networks of an individual as the shell of an enormous building, the chakras are the pillars that bear the building, through which all energy enters and leaves, allowing contact with the world outside the building or body.

Another characteristic of chakras or energy centers is that they serve as influential openings to specific systems in the body, and indeed to the body itself. The influence of the opening is not only determined by the opening itself in the energy field, but also by the fact that the openings are spiral, allowing entry into or exit from the chakra through highly powerful energy gyrations.

Since the purpose of crystal is effectively to create energy gyrations or beams which will penetrate the human body in order to charge or balance the energies therein, the relationship between the crystal and the chakra is of considerable importance. The correct activation of the crystal will create a spiral energy gyration which in turn creates the strongest possible connection between the crystal and the chakra in the human body.

Traditionally, there are seven chakras or energy centers in the human body. These are dispersed along the entire body. Occasionally other opinions may be encountered — some believe that there are eight, thirteen, or twenty-two chakras. However, the common view — particularly in terms of crystals and their use — is that there are seven chakras.

Each chakra is active in and responsible for a particular region, both in physical and mental terms. It therefore follows that each chakra has its own special colors and stones.

An acquaintance with the chakras offers real advantages. First, when we wish to treat a particular problem using a given stone, we will know where to find the most appropriate "gate" through which to administer the treatment. Secondly, and conversely, when we do not know where the problem is or how to treat it, concentrating on the seven chakras means that we will eventually be bound to "strike" the problem and treat it.

We must recall that treatment with crystals occurs by

creating connections between the stone and the body's energy. This may be achieved by placing the stone on or opposite a given chakra, if we know the precise nature of the problem and how to treat it. We can also try to find a general treatment that passes through all the energy fields.

If you encounter a case where treatment occurs while the person is lying on his back, while various stones are passed along the body (in circles, triangles, or other shapes), the attempt being made is to cover all the likely possibilities by "covering" all seven chakras.

Since each chakra has its own unique nature, seven crystals may be used, each relating to a particular chakra. These seven stones are usually placed on a stick, according to the order of the chakras in the body. Such a stick may be used for general treatments.

It is important to note that it is no coincidence that we talk of seven energy centers. Seven is a number with powerful mystical capacities. If we look at a Star of David, for example, we can see that it is divided into seven "points" — the six points of the triangles and the center point. These seven points are the equivalents of the eastern chakras in the western philosophy of body energy.

So if we thought that a recognition of energy centers and their function for charging energies was only an expression of mysterious and exotic eastern philosophy — we were wrong!

As we know, one of the ways to charge the human body with energies is to hold the stone in the left hand and use the right hand to touch a particular part of the body. Suppose that we do not know exactly where a particular problem lies or what stone would be appropriate. Instead of lying on the back and placing stones on the body, we could take the stones one at a time, hold them in our left hand, and use our right hand to touch the seven chakras one after the other.

If this procedure sounds familiar to you, this is no coincidence. For example, this is how the custom developed whereby devout Christians cross themselves before their God.

An understanding of the concept of the chakra and the location of the seven chakras, along with the color and function of each one and the appropriate crystals, is an important stage in getting to know crystals and different types of healing.

We will come to learn that chakras also link healing to the subject of the aura, soothsaying, body and soul, and other concepts from the world of consciousness and the holistic approach to the human body.

The word chakra comes from Sanskrit and means "rotating wheel." The concept of the wheel refers to a large center of spiritual energy; by "turning" the wheel, we create a "gyration" that has the power to absorb other energies. This is where the "energy center" differs from the "energy points," of which hundreds and thousands exist in the human body. In western terms, one might say that the chakra is a junction in the nervous system, while an energy point is the "terminus" of a single nerve.

If we draw a straight line down the human body, from the skull to the end of the spine, we will find the seven chakras along this line. Those who see auras, for example, will see each chakra as a colorful and compact body into and from which a large number of energy lines lead. Some of the systems clustered around the chakras are well known and may be seen with the eye (such as the blood, lymph, or nervous systems), while others are composed of electro-magnetic energy.

When we manage to see the chakras by seeing the aura, we can distinguish them in the form of a colorful flower. The flower resembles a lotus, so that chakras are described as a lotus flower in various positions.

It must be appreciated that in all matters relating to healing, crystals, and the aura, we see the human body as comprising a number of different layers: the physical body, the astral body, the ethereal body, and so on. When we talk about chakras, we usually relate to four different bodies: the physical body, the ethereal body, the emotional body, and the mental body, the last of which is the broadest, encompassing all the other bodies. The chakra permeates and exists in all four bodies; thus it links them and enables simultaneous treatment of the four different levels.

If we compare this to a pin stuck in the body, the pin penetrates all the sections of the skin and is simultaneously in contact with each layer. Thus the pin may be seen as a conduit between the different layers of the skin. The same applies to the chakras, as pipes connecting the different layers of the body.

When we wish to transfer energy from one "body" to another (in the same person), for example to strengthen the physical body and give it the strength to fight disease by transferring to it forces from the mental body of the same person, then the chakra is the most effective channel for this transfer of energy and strength, since it is in simultaneous contact with both these "bodies."

Naturally, when we want to "transfuse" positive energy or "drain" negative energy, the chakra is the most appropriate conduit.

If we examine the chakra through aura vision or by another means of examining energy, we see a circle, wheel, cone, or flower shape, in which strong colored energy moves in a spiral fashion, constantly beating. When the "flower" is very open, there is extensive contact between the chakra and the outside world, and the body is being charged with or losing energy in large quantities (depending on the direction of the gyration). When the flower is closed, the gyration is internal, sometimes self-consuming. The proper balance of each individual depends on the extent to which each chakra is open to the outside, i.e., the extent of contact with external energies, and the direction of the energy gyration within the chakra — i.e., whether the chakra is losing or absorbing energies. We should add that each chakra has its own special type of energy characterized by a given color (marking the channel on which the energy "works").

When all the chakras are balanced and active, we will see in the aura seven colorful flowers along the human body, each slightly open; and in each flower, we see an energetic body similar to a beating heart. The purpose of any type of healing, or of the personal use of crystals, is to reach this state of being.

Crystal is the most effective way to treat chakras and chakra energies, since the nature and form of movement of energy in the chakra and in crystal are very similar. Thus crystal serves as the most effective tool or instrument for tuning, intensifying, or cleansing the energies of the chakras.

We shall now examine the seven different chakras.

The First Chakra

The first chakra is called Muladhara, which means root or base. This chakra is located in the fundament of the body, in the anus. It is important to accept that the anus is in no sense a "dirty" part of the body; in Eastern philosophy, it is an integral part of the human body.

This chakra is responsible for the energy of survival — the ability to create a contact that includes fusion. This chakra links a spiritual capacity with the physical expression of that capacity.

When this opening is blocked, the individual feels

fear, anxiety, anger, and frustration. The physical symptoms of this will include nail-biting, closed fists, violence, and insecurity (and sometimes loss of balance). This may also be expressed in physical damage to various organs in the body, such as the knees, or in arthritis, nervous diseases, and neck pains.

When this chakra is balanced, the individual will be balanced in his or her behavior and moderate in the path he or she chooses.

The dominant color in this area is brown or black. When working on this chakra, use must also be made of the color red. Any stone with black or red radiation will be suitable.

The Second Chakra

This chakra is called Svadhisthana or sacral chakra; it is also known as the "sex chakra." It is located in the pelvis, opposite the pubic region. The name of this chakra means "inside the body," referring to the "privacy" of the human. This chakra is responsible for desire, pleasure, sexuality, and biological continuity. This does not only mean "bodily" functions, however; this area also controls creativity, training, self-realization, and commitment to goals and paths.

When the chakra is blocked, the individual feels confused and restless. Impotence, frigidity, problems in defecation and urination, and back pain may also be encountered. When this chakra is balanced, the individual is brave, conveys charisma and sex appeal to members of the opposite sex, and realizes his or her dreams.

This chakra's color is orange (tending to red). All stones that radiate orange are suitable in treatment, as well as organic stones such as coral and amber.

This chakra is also used for special treatments of sexually-related problems, a method known as "the blossoming lotus of love."

The Third Chakra

The third chakra is called Manipura, which means "the temple of the diamond." In the west, this chakra is known as the "solar plexus" or navel chakra. It is located opposite the navel.

This chakra is responsible for the ego and human development. This is the source of emotions and sensations, of self-will and the use of will to achieve goals. One might say that this is where the human "digests" the outside world and internalizes it in the form of personal feelings.

When this chakra is blocked, the individual cannot find his way in life. When this chakra is balanced, by contrast, the individual finds his place in the world and realizes human conscience while acting within the universe.

The color associated with this chakra is bright yellow, and the appropriate stones are yellow or yellow-white.

This is an important chakra which, if blocked, also effects the other chakras. It is important to treat this point in any case of distress.

The Fourth Chakra

This chakra is called Anhata, which means "the ever-beating drum." In the west, this is known as the heart chakra. It is located in the center of the chest, at heart level.

This is the chakra of love. Some see it as the central chakra, balancing the entire body. When this chakra is balanced and open, it exerts a positive influence on all the other chakras. When it is blocked, physical symptoms such as breathing difficulties, high blood pressure, heart and lung problems may result.

An open chakra enables the individual to join in love with others, and to feel for another heart. It is also important, however, to emphasize the importance of this chakra for the individual's physical well-being, as indicated by the fact that the color associated with this chakra is green. Stones with any shade of green influence this chakra.

The Fifth Chakra

This chakra is known as Vishuddha or the throat chakra. The original name means "full of purity." It is located in the throat, at the bottom of the pharynx (it is therefore connected to the mouth). This chakra is associated with communication, creativity and self-expression — i.e., forms of inner expression through external manifestations. Some say that this chakra relates to the individual's expression of his own truth.

When this chakra is balanced — and in this case, this essentially means when it is open — there is a connection between the individual and the supreme force, and the human is aware of the laws of creation, enabling him or her to reach purity and maintain spiritual serenity in any situation. When this chakra is blocked, the physical expressions are mainly muscle tension, inflammations (colds), and problems with vision and hearing.

The color associated with this chakra is blue, and this is the radiation needed from stones used to treat this point. It is very difficult to balance this particular chakra, and considerable knowledge is required in order to do so.

The Sixth Chakra

This is the Ajana chakra, or "brow chakra". In the west, it is known as the third-eye chakra. It is located in the center of the forehead, between the eyebrows.

This chakra opens a gate to the subconscious or intuition, in simple terms. When balanced (open), this area enables soothsaying, and the location of knowledge appropriate for making the right decisions. When this chakra is blocked, the individual may suffer from blindness, headaches, nightmares, and "silliness."

The color associated with this chakra is violet, and this is the radiation needed from stones used to treat this area. It is difficult to balance this chakra — a high level of self-awareness is required.

The Seventh Chakra

This chakra is known as Sahasrara or Sahasharta, "the lotus flower of the thousand petals." In the west, it is known as the crown chakra. It is located at the crown of the head (where babies have their soft spot), and it is parallel to the first chakra in the anus.

This chakra is responsible for supreme awareness, the acquisition of higher wisdom, and identification with the universe and with God. This is a supremely "spiritual" chakra. An open and balanced chakra will enable the individual to see, understand, and love the supreme light. When this chakra is blocked, the individual will feel depression, boredom in everyday life, and a sense of purposelessness. This chakra connects the human with the upper worlds.

The color associated with this chakra is bright white (representing the entire rainbow). The main stone used to treat this chakra is diamond.

Meditation and the Blessing of the Stone

When we speak of the blessing of the stone or the crystal, we relate to a formula with two components. On the one hand there is the crystal or the stone we use, and on the other hand, there is the ability to use the property of the stone to our benefit in the widest sense — physically, mentally, and spiritually.

The ability to utilize the properties of the stone is one shared by all humans, even those who are unaware of or who deny these properties. However, only relatively few people have achieved a level of ability sufficient to enable them to understand and exploit the properties of the stone without the "development" or "training" of this human potential.

The tool to be used in developing the ability to utilize the properties of stones is one that is familiar to many of us: meditation.

Meditation essentially means the raising of the individual's mental capacity in order to enable it to control his or her physical and spiritual sides. Through meditation humans can raise their mental abilities to unknown heights, freeing themselves from the limitations of the five conventional senses and penetrating the subconscious and the higher world of enlightenment.

It is obvious that humans have much to gain from acquainting themselves with meditation and from rational and wise use of this technique. It is equally obvious, however, that no good will come of meditation performed with a negative objective or goal. In all matters relating to meditation, we must remember that the main factor determining the destiny of the process is our own intention.

Another point to recall is that meditation may be likened to rain falling on parched soil, stimulating a tiny seed or nucleus, helping it to grow and realize its destiny. This is just what meditation does for the individual — stimulating the soul and helping the individual to realize his or her destiny and to put into practice supreme capabilities. However, all this depends on the existence of the seed or nucleus; only when such a seed exists within the individual can meditation help it to grow!

It is important to remember this point, since people often try to use meditation, or other less positive aids (such as drugs, asceticism, or blind faith, for example) to obtain properties for which no "seed" exists within their own personality.

Without the presence of such a seed, however tiny, meditation cannot help in that particular field. No person can be other than who they are!

In this respect, meditation is like a crystal: it needs a nucleus around which to form, like a drop of rain or the aura of a human. Even if we do everything we can to cast abundant green light on a person's aura, we cannot succeed if his or her existing aura does not contain even the tiniest fragment of green!

When properly performed, meditation evokes the following:

* It maximizes and enhances the individual's personal capabilities. Some people compare meditation with a pencil sharpener. While everything is there in the pencil, it is useless without the sharpener to remove the unwanted wood.

* Meditation helps people to free themselves of the pressures that distort and stunt personal growth and expression. In this respect meditation has something to offer everyone.

* Meditation strengthens our ability to resist and cope with the problems caused by stress, depression, and tension. Even if people are unable or unwilling to avoid the causes of stress, meditation enhances their power to resist these causes.

* Meditation helps us expand and increase our range of vision or thought. While meditation cannot force the tasks and problems we face to retreat or vanish, we find that they diminish in importance in the new picture. People see their problems and tasks from a different, more rational and realistic perspective. Although nothing has changed in our daily life, what used to be a mountain of problems is now a small hill.

    * Meditations helps us to allocate human resources more effectively and appropriately. In other words, people find that meditation enables them to use the sources available to them (even if those have not been increased) to accomplish a larger number of tasks.

    * Meditation develops our capacity to achieve spiritual enlightenment, i.e., a higher level of self- and general awareness. Senses are sharpened, physical and mental alertness are intensified, and quality of life in general is improved.

When the use of meditation is combined with crystals, the process and results of meditation are strengthened enormously. The equation also works the other way round: when the use of crystals is augmented by meditation, the stone's blessing is reinforced and achieves its full potential.

In fact, the stone's blessing calls for different forms of meditation with stones. The combination of crystals and meditation leads to the best results.

Before moving on we should note that everyone can experiment with combining meditation and crystals. In so doing, the following general instructions should be kept in mind:

When you want to strengthen the intellect or "cerebral" capacity using inner energy drawn from the body itself, use quartz crystal during meditation.

When you want to strengthen spiritual meditation,

facilitate communication, and ascend the spiritual spiral leading to the upper worlds (taking the "elevator to heaven"), use amethyst.

When you want to achieve harmony and peace between body and spirit, use your own personal birth stone (based on the zodiac sign in your birth chart).

Use the following table:
Aries – diamond, ruby, red jasper
Taurus – sapphire, lapis lazuli
Gemini – citrin, yellow agate
Cancer – pearl, moonstone
Leo – tiger's eye, agate
Virgo – green jasper, sardonyx
Libra – sapphire, aquamarine
Scorpio – ruby, opal, red jasper
Sagittarius – topaz
Capricorn – turquoise, smokey quartz
Aquarius – amethyst
Pisces – moonstone, rose quartz

In selecting the stone to use, we should recall that it must undergo a process of cleansing, charging, and personal programming before being used. After taking the stone (and ourselves) through this process of adaptation, we are ready to begin meditation.

There are a variety of methods for meditation, but the first step for any method is relaxation. After the stage of relaxation, any one of dozens of meditation methods used around the world may be chosen.

We shall review here a number of methods that are widespread in the Western world. No one method is preferable to another, and the methods appear in no particular order. **All of the methods are based on the use of crystals together with meditation**.

Each method is listed on its own, but specific stages are detailed only the first time they appear (e.g. inhalation/exhalation). It is therefore worth reading through the methods as they appear before selecting the most appropriate technique for yourself.

Meditation using inner concentration

1. Choose a quiet place where you can spend time without interruptions, telephone calls, etc.
2. Sit comfortably, preferably in the middle of the room.
3. Hold your personal crystal in your left hand, with the point raised parallel to your thumb (this is what is meant when we say that the crystal should be "pointed upward").
4. Close your eyes.
5. Begin to breathe in and out slowly and regularly. Try to reach a situation where there is a count of three between each inhalation and exhalation: inhale — one, two, three — exhale — one, two, three — inhale...

6. When you reach the correct rhythm without actually counting, you will feel that you are leaving behind external thoughts and interference.

7. Remain in this state for some time, as long as no external thought or obstacle is bothering you.

8. Once you can remain in this state for 7 to 10 minutes, this is a sign that you have learned to meditate using this method.

This meditation should be performed once a day, preferably at a fixed time. The longer you continue to practice this method, the easier and more effective it becomes.

Meditation using focused vision

1. Choose a quiet place where you can spend some time without being disturbed. Sit comfortably on a mattress or chair, with a table or raised surface of any kind in front of you.

2. Place your personal crystal in the center of the table, with the point facing toward you.

3. Look at the crystal. Focus your vision and make sure to breathe regularly with a set rhythm between each inhalation and exhalation.

4. Focus your gaze on the crystal. You may well "see" fluctuations in the crystal and feel that your vision is blurring. At a certain stage, you will feel an urge to close your eyes. Do so!

5. With your eyes closed, recall the picture of the crystal in your inner vision.

6. Once you can see the crystal with your eyes closed, you are in a state of meditation.

7. Continue to meditate for as long as you can see the crystal in your "mind's eye." Once the picture of the crystal blurs or disappears, open your eyes and finish the meditation session.

This meditation last 4-7 minutes, "net" — i.e. the period of time when you should see the picture of the crystal with your eyes closed. If you close your eyes and the picture of the crystal blurs or disappears, do not try to repeat the exercise that day!

After about ten days, you will become familiar with this method and the picture of the crystal will no longer blur. You may replace the crystal occasionally, but each replacement may require a period of adjustment with meditation beginning again from the first steps.

Meditation using light imaging

1. Choose a quiet place, sit comfortably, and hold your personal crystal in your left hand, with the point parallel to your thumb.

2. Close your eyes and begin a fixed rhythm of inhalation/exhalation.

3. Imagine a ball of light appearing opposite your third eye (forehead).

4. Through controlled breathing, draw the light in to your mouth. Feel the light spreading throughout your body. At this stage, note that the emphasis is on inhalation, so that the exhalation does not expel the light.

5. Reach a state where you are completely "enlightened" and feel a warm sensation in your body. You must be in such a state for three consecutiv minutes.

6. Return the light to the external ball by concentrating in exhalation. Although the light leaves the body, you will still feel warm.

7. Open your eyes and continue to breathe regularly until you feel that the body has cooled down again.

8. It is a good idea to take a shower in running water after completing this meditation.

This meditation, which is based on imagery, is powerful and effective, although it takes some time to learn to use it for our needs.

You may attempt this method several times, even if you fail the first time.

Meditation using crystal focusing

In this method, we "allow" the crystals to guide us to the correct manner of meditation. To attempt this method, a number of similar crystals (3, 5, or 7) are needed.

1. Choose a suitable room where you will not be disturbed, and place a mat or thin mattress on the floor. If you meditate on the bare floor, sweep it gently before sitting down. To use this method, you must be on the same level as the crystals.

2. Sit in the middle of the room and place the crystals around you in the form of a triangle (3 crystals), a pentagon (5 crystals), or a circle (7 crystals). Make sure that you are in the center, and that all the points are facing the center.

3. Close your eyes and begin a slow rhythm of inhalation and exhalation.

4. You must remain in this state for a relatively long time, since the crystals have to interact with each other before the influence reaches you. This meditation takes approximately 15 to 25 minutes.

5. On completing the meditation, it is important to clean the crystals thoroughly.

This meditation is good for people who find it difficult to achieve the state of deep relaxation essential for any type of meditation. This meditation is not ended when you open your eyes, move, or change your breathing rhythm.

Meditation using a picture mantra

To use this method, you must have a "picture mantra" — a picture or drawing that expresses an idea for you. This is usually a geometrical form such as a triangle inside a circle, a circle inside a square, a Star of David inside a circle, an inverted pentagon inside a regular pentagram, and so on.

1. Choose a suitable place where you will not be disturbed.
2. Sit opposite the mantra, holding your crystal in both palms (it does not matter what direction the point is facing).
3. Fix your gaze on the picture mantra, breathing in and out at a fixed rhythm.
4. After a short while you will feel that the crystal in your hand is merging with the mantra!
5. At this stage you are in a state of meditation, and will usually close your eyes. Remain in this state for about ten minutes.

This is a powerful form of meditation, though it is not easy to achieve. Regular daily practice strengthens its impact.

When you change the crystal or the picture mantra, this sometimes creates dissonance making it difficult or impossible to achieve meditation.

(This meditation is also used with the assistance of appropriate music, usually with a very strong and repetitive rhythm. The method is the same in principle, except that instead of the picture mantra, you open your ears and soul to the sounds of the aural mantra).

Note that all these forms of meditation take place when the individual is alone in the room. Group meditation methods also exist, but we shall not discuss these here. In any case, two or more people may meditate as individuals while being in the same room at the same time — as long as they do not disturb each other or distract each other's attention from the meditation.

In order to enable the stone's blessing to be expressed in full, it is important to become familiar with the various methods used for meditating with crystals and to choose the one that will help you achieve the best results.

Dozens more methods exist for using crystals in meditation. The truth is that any practice of carrying or holding crystals is connected to a lesser or greater extent with meditation. Over time, each individual will find that he chooses the most appropriate method of meditation for himself or herself and for his or her personal crystal, whether by using one of the methods described here, by combining several of them, or by finding another method.

Placing Crystals

These days, everyone encounters crystals. Directly or indirectly, in jewelry or charms, in alternative medicine or in consciousness-raising, we find crystals. People who collect precious stones discover the properties of the stone or crystal and use them for themselves and for others. In place of the intuitive collection of crystals based on their shape, color, or shine (not forgetting the question of price!), people begin at some stage in their life to learn more about the properties of stones, about the chakras in the human body, about awareness, aura, and colors. Thus the simple habit of collection is transformed into an entire philosophy that develops human consciousness to its most expanded forms.

In the learning process about crystals there are also stages. The starting point is usually a familiarization with crystals and the different characteristics attributed to each stone. This is followed by study of chakras and later by the ways crystals can be connected to the body or to a specific problem we wish to solve.

When the learning process evolves to learning about the placement of crystals, we have moved onto a higher plane of crystal usage. This level requires a knowledge of crystals and of the meaning of the body — body, spirit, and soul in the widest sense — as well as an understanding of the flow of electromagnetic energy between the different crystals and between the crystals and the body.

The easy way to learn about placing crystals (though it is not a way we recommend) is to learn by rote tables that explain where to place each crystal. However, in the end such learning is not effective. Everyone using crystals must realize that there is a variety of methods available for placing and combining crystals, for reinforcing or moderating the strength of a given crystal, and for embedding crystals in energy. Learning by rote without comprehension cannot help us find the best way for ourselves to transmit energy from the crystal to the body.

Only by learning the various methods can we choose the most appropriate crystals for ourselves and for our own goal (or effectively use the crystals we already possess).

In order to understand the placement of crystals, and **without discussing the classification of crystals for different purposes**, we must first understand something important about the structure of crystals.

Try to imagine (or even take in your hands) two magnets of different strengths. The magnets may be placed so that their poles stick to each other as if with glue; they may be placed so that the poles will reject each other. We can place pins on a table and put the weaker magnet near them, in order to arrange the pins in a given form. Placing the stronger magnet alone on the table will produce a different form. Put the weaker magnet back on the table and place the stronger one near it, and the pins will once again change their arrangement!

That is, as far as the pins (the body we wish to influence) are concerned, it makes a difference whether the first, weaker magnet is alone or if another, stronger magnet is also present. Although both magnets work according to the same principles, combining them creates something different than each one on its own. We might add that combining magnets produces something that differs from a 2+2=4 situation. In other words, if we combine the forces of two magnets into a single magnet and place this by the pins, the arrangement produced will be different from that produced in the case of the weaker magnet on its own, or the stronger magnet on its own, or **both magnets together on the table**. We would obtain a fourth option not previously present.

In this respect, crystals are just like magnets. If we place two crystals together, even two that are identical, we receive another structure of crystalline influence quite different from that of each crystal on its own, and not necessarily a simple mathematical combination of the powers of both crystals.

Moreover, even if we use identical crystals, the shape in which we arrange the crystals is extremely important — for example, in a straight line or circle. When using different crystals of various strengths and fields of influence, the importance of the arrangement in which we place the crystals increases significantly.

In order to learn to utilize the characteristics of crystals, we must recognize the different ways in which they may be placed. We shall discuss here eight principal ways of placing crystals (which may effectively be used to compose all of the remaining possible arrangements).

Our discussion here relates only to the placement of crystals. At this stage, we are not interested in which particular crystals are being placed (this has been discussed throughout the book). We assume that those who have reached this stage of familiarity with crystals will already be familiar with the properties of the particularly crystal — properties which they now wish to "nurture" and use to the full.

Whenever we say <u>upward</u> we mean toward the person's head (crystals are placed on the human body, usually when someone is lying on their back). When we say <u>downward</u>, we mean pointing toward the person's legs.

The arrows in the diagrams always refer to the direction of energy flow. That is, the electromagnetic energy of the crystal located by the head of the arrow will increase, while the energy of the crystal at the "tail" of the arrow (where the arrow begins) will decrease.

(In the diagrams, the darker circle is the crystal accumulating energy; the gray circle is a crystal maintaining or balancing energy; and the white circle is a crystal losing substantial energy. The arrow shows the direction of energy flow.)

1. The simplest form of all is **the standing pair** — two crystals, one of which points up to the head, and the other down to the legs. The higher crystal enhances its power.

When we "lay down" the pair of crystals, we receive **the lying pair** formation: two crystals, side by side, across the body. Here there is no up and down, and the movement is two-way. Both crystals reinforce each other (though at a low intensity relative to the standing pair formation).

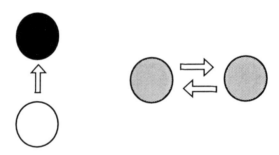

2. **Crystal trio:** when there is a vertical line of crystals, the upper crystal is strengthened, but the middle one does not increase in strength.

When a crystal trio is lying down, only the middle crystal is strengthened (at great intensity), since it receives energy from both the left and right sides.

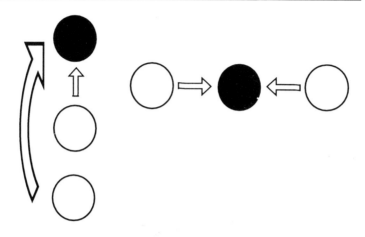

3. **The climbing seven** is an arrangement of crystals opposite the seven chakras (usually, seven different crystals will be used, each one appropriate for the chakra opposite which it is placed). The uppermost stone achieves maximum energetic enhancement by this method. The middle stone is also strengthened, under the influence of the three lower stones. Since this placement includes a sequence of energies of a large number of crystals, the increased strength does not significantly reduce the strength of the other crystals. This method is convenient and useful for general purposes.

(In the east, some people use nine crystals instead of seven — this is the "crystal nine" mentioned in various works. When nine crystals are used, the three lowest ones must be of the same type, and preferably the same size. We recommend a maximum of seven crystals, ideally different from each other and appropriate to the relevant chakra.)

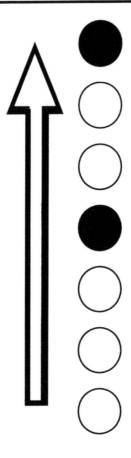

4. **The crystal triangle** is an arrangement of three crystals in triangular form. The upper crystal is strongly reinforced in a balanced and different manner by each of the other crystals. This formation is useful mainly as a component in another placement method or methods.

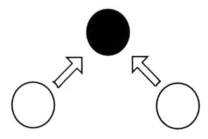

5. **The stone cross** or **crystal square** is a formation using five crystals placed in the form of a cross, with the fifth stone in the center. In this formation, only the stone in the center is strengthened (very intensely). Extreme caution must be employed when using this formation.

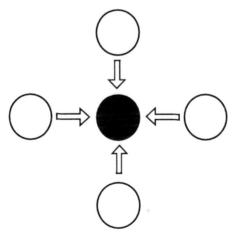

6. **The crystal pentagram** is a formation where the crystals are placed in the form of a pentagram. The upper stone draws considerable and balanced force from both the lower ones; the two middle crystals do not send

energy to the upper crystal, but strengthen one another, serving as a base for the upper stone. This method is effective for meditation and for consciousness raising.

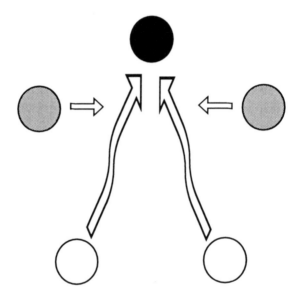

7. **The Star of David** is a good method for balancing bodily energies. The upper crystal receives energy from two crystals, and **the lower crystal receives energy from two crystals**. This combination leads to an almost perfect combination in developing integrated energy.

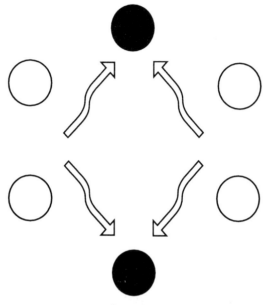

8. **The crystal circle** is a more complex formation where an **uneven number of crystals** from five up are placed in a circle.

When crystals are placed in a circle, energy is strengthened in an counter-clockwise direction (it is therefore important to put each crystal in the correct place in order to give its neighbor the energy it requires). This method is actually an infinite empowering movement that will be frozen or halted only because of the "seeping" of energy outward from the circle.

An additional crystal (usually of a generator type) may also be placed in the center of the circle. In this case, the energy is concentrated within the circle, and rather than having energy "seep" out, we achieve a tremendous focusing of energy in addition to that which occurs around the circle itself. This formation produces an enormous cluster of energy and must be used with caution.

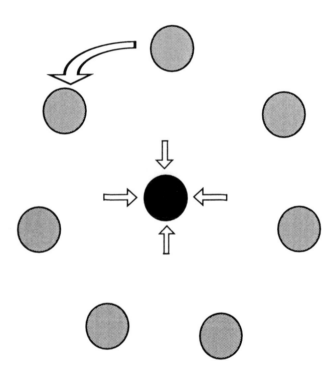

Laying Crystals

When we lay crystals on the body (and we shall relate here to the ordinary quartz crystal, the basic crystal in any formation for healing or meditation), a number of fixed formations may be used. (See: placing crystals).

When a person becomes trained in the use of crystals, they will choose the formation for laying crystals according to their own needs and properties. Those who do not clearly know how to use crystals should consult a healer or consultant in order to place them or have them placed.

We know that one basic method for laying crystals creates connections between the crystal, the chakra, and the color. Opposite each chakra, we place a crystal that is of appropriate **color**, thus reinforcing the electromagnetic field exerted on the chakra.

We shall now discuss two different methods for laying crystals that may be used by anyone in any situation. One only must be sure to use the crystals mentioned here, and not to improvise. Both methods take place when the person is lying on their back, their legs open slightly, on a mattress or blanket, with their arms by the side of their body and pressed to the mattress, and their gaze focused directly above their head.

The path of seven

The first method is based on the number seven, by way of analogy to the seven chakras (but under no circumstances parallel to the chakras).

The first crystal, a clear, translucent quartz with a single, clearly-defined point (single terminated), is placed on the mattress a hand's width from the head, with **the point clearly facing away from the head**.

Two additional crystals, also with clearly defined points, are placed a hand's width from the shoulders, firstly on the person's left side and then on the right. Here, too, **the points face upward towards the head**.

These three crystals create a triangle of energy influencing the upper chakras. The better these three crystals are coordinated, the stronger their influence.

Similarly, we take three more crystals with clearly defined points. The first is placed between the feet, about a hand's width from each foot, with **the point facing down away from the feet**. We then place the next two crystals on either side of the body, alongside and one hand's width away from the hands, with **the points facing down**.

These three crystals create the lower energy triangle, which influences the lower chakras. The better these three crystals are coordinated (without reference to the upper trio), the stronger the influence.

We must now take a seventh crystal, which **must be a double-pointed** (double terminated)**, large and beautiful quartz**. This crystal is placed on the heart, with **one point facing upward to the head, and the other down to the feet**. This crystal connects and balances the energy flow between the two energy triangles or circuits.

The path of seven is a general formation effective for any type of healing and meditation. Various changes or variations exist on this method, but the bottom line is that this is the recommended method for drawing energy from crystals!

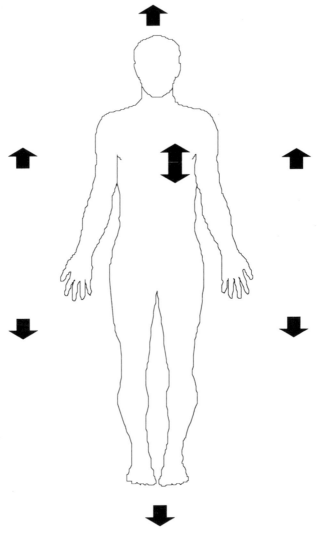

Diagram of the path of seven

The path of twelve

This is a highly powerful method, used in a similar manner to the path of seven, but offering increased intensity. In this case we use twelve similar crystals, all **with a single, clearly defined point** (single terminated). Note that the person lies in the same position as described above.

One crystal is placed above the head, with the point facing up. A second crystal is placed below the feet, **also with the point facing up**.

The remaining crystals are sorted into pairs, which should be identical or as similar as possible, and placed on either side of the body, firstly to the left and then to the right, parallel to the shoulders, elbows, hands, knees, and feet. The crystals are placed in a straight line, with **all the points facing up toward the head**.

The diagrams will facilitate an understanding of the entire picture. When using either of these methods to lay crystals, make sure to choose clean, clear quartz crystals, and to use crystals of similar size (with the exception of the double-pointed crystal in the path of seven, which may be up to twice the size of the others).

After laying the crystals, you must lie in a state of complete relaxation in order to draw in the crystal energy, for not more than twenty minutes. After use, the crystals should be properly cleansed and stored.

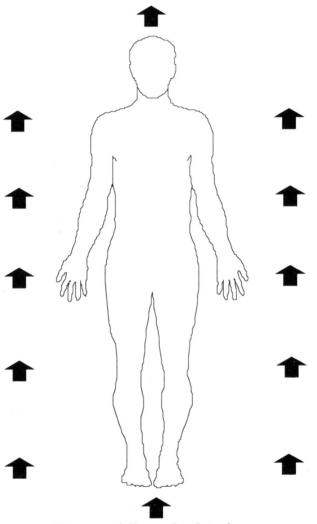

Diagram of the path of twelve